THE IMPASSIBILITY OF GOD

T0382167

THE IMPASSIBILITY OF GOD

A SURVEY OF CHRISTIAN THOUGHT

by

J. K. MOZLEY, B.D.

Warden of St Augustine's House, Reading
Lecturer of Leeds Parish Church

CAMBRIDGE

AT THE UNIVERSITY PRESS

MCMXXVI

CAMBRIDGE
UNIVERSITY PRESS

University Printing House, Cambridge CB2 8BS, United Kingdom

Cambridge University Press is part of the University of Cambridge.

It furthers the University's mission by disseminating knowledge in the pursuit of education, learning and research at the highest international levels of excellence.

www.cambridge.org
Information on this title: www.cambridge.org/9781107438187

© Cambridge University Press 1926

First published 1926
First paperback edition 2014

A catalogue record for this publication is available from the British Library

ISBN 978-1-107-43818-7 Paperback

PREFACE

The present volume has grown out of a task assigned to me during the meetings of the Archbishops' Doctrinal Commission in September 1924, to prepare a historical statement on the subject of the doctrine of the Impassibility of God. How considerable an undertaking it would be, I had no idea at the time; but when I set to work upon it, it grew, I may say, almost of its own accord. More and still more relevant material from the Fathers and elsewhere kept turning up, till I realized that I could neither finish the work as soon as was desirable, nor restrict it to a statement of manageable dimensions, suitable for circulation in type to my fellow-members. Then it occurred to me that, as it had reached a respectable size, and had entailed much more work than either I or (if I may say so) the Commission had foreseen, it might, without impropriety, be submitted at Cambridge, in the hope that it and I would be approved for a doctorate in divinity. In this, I am glad to say, it was successful, and as I had found it no easy matter to find time to prepare a thesis which could be offered with a view to that degree, I am the more grateful to the Commission for the labour which was imposed upon me.

In the body of the work I have suggested or implied that there has been an astonishing lack of serious attention to the subject of Impassibility. Many theologians have, in recent times, touched upon it, and there has been a good deal of passionate reaction from the doctrine.

But it is very curious that of monographs avowedly devoted to the question we have, as far as I have been able to discover, only two, the work of Gregory Thaumaturgus in the third century, *De passibili et impassibili in Deo*, and the work of Dr Marshall Randles, at the end of the nineteenth, *The Blessed God. Impassibility.* How it comes about that there is no classic German monograph to lighten the labours of other students, I cannot imagine. If there is one, and I have missed it, I apologise to its author: but I am still inclined to think that he does not exist. And in English, for the history of the doctrine, the student will have begun and ended his course with Principal R. S. Franks in the *Encyclopaedia of Religion and Ethics, s.v.* "Passibility and Impassibility." It is an article which would show him the lie of the land, but without exhibiting in any detail the features of the country.

As to the present work, I wish to express my regret for two omissions. Of Bishop F. J. McConnell's volume entitled *Is God Limited?* and published in the Crown Theological Library I have said nothing. I had fully intended to make use of it, and it was quite without intention on my part that, when the text was finished and had gone off to Cambridge, Bishop McConnell was not travelling in the company of the other eminent modern authors who were occupying their places. So to this extent I try to compensate for my omission by referring the reader to chapter xxiii in Bishop McConnell's book, with the title "The Wealth of the Divine Feeling." He will discover a very definite repudiation of the doctrine of impassibility, and will class Bishop McConnell with Canon Streeter, Mr Studdert-Kennedy, Dr Douglas White and others—whether for approval or for disapproval.

The other omission is of a different character, and I should never have realized it but for a question put to me by the Rev. E. G. Selwyn. What he asked was, in effect, this—"have you said anything about the bearing upon the doctrine of impassibility of Christian belief in the Holy Spirit?" That seems to me a very valuable question, and the omission is serious. For our Christian belief in the Holy Spirit is not simply another way of expressing our belief in the immanence of God. If that were all, I should not feel that I had been guilty of an omission; for though the word immanence is used infrequently in the following pages, the idea for which it stands is certainly not absent. But even in a historical study which does not pretend to be an examination of what may or may not be regarded as true, definite reference ought to have been made to the eighth chapter of Romans, and something suggested as to its implications.

The book is concerned with what has become a controversial—sometimes a fiercely controversial—question. It is a presentation of evidence, and, in the closing pages, an attempt to show what are the problems that must be investigated before the question can be satisfactorily answered. At least, with regard to these problems some line must be taken; it is only through them that one can scientifically approach the discussion of impassibility. Most people who are at all interested in the problems of philosophy and theology will have some idea where they stand. If I have said nothing about my own beliefs, that is not, I hope, through any wish to shirk responsibility, but in order that the collected evidence may make its own impression on the mind of the reader without any middleman's interference from the author of the book.

To the Syndics of the Cambridge University Press, to Mr S. C. Roberts, the Secretary of the Press, and to those careful proof-readers and printers to whom the book owes so much, I would express my very grateful thanks.

J. K. M.

19 *August* 1926

CONTENTS

CONCLUSION

THE IMPASSIBILITY OF GOD
A SURVEY OF CHRISTIAN THOUGHT

INTRODUCTION

THE purpose of this study is primarily historical. It is an attempt to state what has been believed with regard to God's incapacity for suffering, rather than to examine and evaluate the belief itself. No such study can, of course, be purely in the nature of a record. The causes of beliefs and the ways in which they have been stated must throw some light upon the beliefs, must serve to some extent as a criterion for appraising their worth. And much harm results from inattention to the historical background. Whether the idea of a "suffering God" be true or false, exponents of this conception would have been well advised to discuss it in the light of the Christian tradition.

THE OLD TESTAMENT

We may start with the Old Testament. Two facts are obvious and relevant; first, that Hebrew thought, at least from the period of the writing prophets, always involved what we must call a transcendental element in its notion of God, secondly that in the Old Testament there is hardly anything we can call metaphysical speculation. The transcendentalism is to be seen in the radical distinction between God and the world, and God and man. Pantheism, whether in a materialistic or spiritualistic form, such as proved attractive in various aspects of Greek thought, was wholly alien to the Jew until he came under the influence of Greek ideas, and then we connect it with Alexandria not with Palestine. Nor can we say that this transcendence is of the character of such a superhumanity as is manifested in the Homeric deities of Olympus. On the contrary, it is bound up with the thought of moral distinction. Here we recognize something of fundamental importance in connexion with Jewish religion, and we cannot date its beginnings with the eighth century. Professor Wheeler Robinson emphasizes the anthropomorphism of early Jewish thought, especially as found in J, but in the earlier period he sees that sense of God's moral character upon which Amos, Hosea and Isaiah laid such stress. He refers to the cases of Nathan and Elijah, and to the evidence of the Book of the Covenant, while of J and E he says that they "similarly show a moral conception of Yahweh that effectually unites the period of David with the eighth century[1]."

On the other hand, the unspeculative character of the Hebrew mind prevented the prophets and writers of Israel from feeling those difficulties in connexion with the notion of divine personality of which the

---

[1] *Religious Ideas of the Old Testament*, p. 67; cf. Prof. W. G. Jordan in Peake's *Commentary*, article "The Religion of Israel." Like Professor Robinson he connects the moral character of God with the relationship which unites God and His people. "Though the idea of a 'covenant' between Yahweh and Israel has been expanded and presented from different points of view by later prophetic and literary activity, it is no doubt here in a simple form and has a real *ethical* character... Here, though the situation is a narrow national one, it is at a higher plane than any mere 'nature' worship or absolutely local deity" (p. 84).

Greek thinkers were conscious, and which comes to striking expression in one of the fragments of Xenophanes, and from hesitating to make use of highly anthropomorphic expressions. What we need to attend to is not the language of J and its ascription to God of bodily characteristics (*e.g.* Gen. iii, 8; viii, 21), but the picture of a mental and emotional life in God which is common to the prophets as well as to the earlier documents. God was absolutely other than man in His perfect holiness and in His eternal being. Isaiah's vision is the classic passage for the first; God's assurance, "As I live for ever," in the Song of Moses (Deut. xxxii, 40) is one of the many instances of the second. But these convictions were in no way incompatible with feelings being attributed to God, even as to man. God is indeed constant, trustworthy, faithful to His covenant and promises; it can be said "I, the Lord, change not; therefore ye, O sons of Jacob, are not consumed" (Mal. iii, 6), but we are in the presence here of no such metaphysical immutability as belongs, for instance, to Aristotle's notion of God. Love, joy, anger, jealousy, "repentance," are all ascribed to God, differing from the corresponding feelings in men only by their conformity with God's perfect righteousness. There is nothing surprising in the fact that both in the primitive and in the late literature of the Old Testament we read of the sorrow or the affliction of God. In Genesis vi, 6 God is "grieved at his heart" because He has created a race which has morally corrupted itself; in Judges x, 16 the soul of the Lord is said to be "grieved for the misery of Israel," while Isaiah lxiii, 9 gives us the most comprehensive statement of all, "In all their affliction he was afflicted," to which is added the saying that despite God's care for His people, "they grieved his holy spirit."

It is just because the metaphysical interest of the Greek was absent from the Jew that we are precluded from the attempt to discover precisely what this picture of God's emotional life meant to the Jew. Schultz in his *Old Testament Theology*[1] devotes a very interesting section to it, but though one may entirely agree with him that the Old Testament epithets "offer certainly in an inadequate form, but still in the only possible one, that which is more important for religion than any philosophical speculations about God," though one may see in the language of the prophets stress laid upon "the full personality of a living God who feels and wills," there seems to be overmuch rationalization when Schultz goes on to show how "the incongruity of form, inseparable from such expressions, is easily explained away," how God's jealousy means that He is not indifferent to human love, while "His wrath and hatred, taken in connexion with His gracious power, are standing expressions for the self-asserting majesty of His living essence." Such may be our interpretation of the picture, but it is dangerous to read it back into an earlier age. We are conscious of a problem; was it so with Amos, Isaiah and the other "theologians" of Israel?

THE NEW TESTAMENT

Nor do we pass into a new atmosphere when we turn from the Old Testament to the New. Principal Franks seems, indeed, to find a strengthening of the earlier

[1] II, pp. 108–10 (Eng. tr.).

conception when he argues that "the fundamental New Testament doctrine of God's Fatherhood suggests the very reverse of His impassibility[1]." Certainly it is true that whether we turn to the teaching of our Lord, or to the Epistles of St Paul, or to the Epistle to the Hebrews, or to the Johannine writings, the old implications attaching to the idea of God's full personal life remain. Especially must we pay attention to the fact that in the New Testament God's attitude to man can be so differently described. God is love, and in His love He gives His Son for the salvation of men. He would have all men to be saved. He is ever ready to welcome home the repentant sinner. Nevertheless His wrath is as plain in the Parables of the Kingdom as it is in the Pauline theology, and we cannot evade the conclusion that to this extent change is conceived of as actual in God, that wrath can give place to the free exercise of love. Ritschl's attempt to evacuate of objective reality the New Testament conception of the wrath of God, especially in his argument that our judgments of experience are irrelevant to something which can be truly appreciated only from the "view-point of eternity," that is, from an understanding of God's eternal purpose to save men, still seems to me "astonishing[2]."

In the article already mentioned Principal Franks records the dependence of Dr Charles Hodge, the most eminent systematic theologian of the Princeton Calvinistic school, upon one proof-text Jas. i, 17[3] for a New

[1] In *Encyc. Rel. and Eth.*, article "Passibility and Impassibility," vol. ix, p. 658.   [2] As in my *Ritschlianism*, p. 210.
[3] The Father of lights, with whom can be no variation, neither shadow that is cast by turning.

Testament doctrine of the immutability of God. This is one definite proof-text; nevertheless, it is proper to bring into consideration the doctrine of God's eternal purposes, as set forth in the Epistle to the Ephesians, though it must not be applied after the manner of Ritschl. As to God's impassibility, apart from such adverse implications as have been found in the character of God as Father, and as arise from whatever suggests that man's conduct affects God, we have the nearest approach to Isaiah lxii, 9, 11 in a passage, similar in terminology to, if not directly dependent upon, the latter of those two verses, where St Paul gives the command "Grieve not the Holy Spirit of God." But when one asks what the significance of such a passage was to the writer, one is bound to remember the wide difference between a context of religious exhortation and a context of philosophical discussion. Moreover, if either context is sharply isolated, there is grave danger of one-sidedness, and, therefore, of inadequacy. A passage such as 1 Tim. vi, 16[1] would seem, in itself, to suggest a conception of God conformable to the presuppositions of Hellenic transcendentalism, but it would be dangerous to draw any very definite conclusions based on such a view of the text. It would be equally rash to suppose that the best reading in Acts xx, 28, "the church of God which he purchased with his own blood," gave any support to Patripassian conclusions. Language of a liturgical or devotional character must not be pressed into the service of theological theory.

[1] Dwelling in light unapproachable, whom no man has seen, nor can see.

CHAPTER I

The History of the Doctrine of Impassibility

I. FROM THE APOSTOLIC FATHERS TO IRENAEUS

Two convictions, of theological and controversial as well as of religious importance, are imbedded in the Pauline and Johannine writings respectively. The first is that at the centre of the Gospel stands the Cross not of a man, but of the Son of God who had emptied Himself, taken upon Himself the form of a servant and given Himself to death for men; the second is that Jesus, who is the Son of God, has come in the flesh, a coming which is also described, with direct reference to the Passion, as a coming "in the blood." This emphasis is only partially carried forward into the second century. Ignatius is the nearest in feeling to the New Testament. The intense fervour of his devotion to Christ appears in such passages as "Suffer me to follow the example of the passion of my God[1]," and "having kindled your brotherly task by the blood of God[2]." But the balanced, antithetical statement of *ad Polyc.* 3 shows that we must not attribute to him views of a suffering God outside of the sphere of the Incarnation. "Wait," he says, "for him who is above seasons, timeless, invisible, who for our sakes became visible, who cannot be touched, who cannot suffer, who for our sakes accepted suffering, who in every way endured for our sakes." The thought clearly is that Christ in the incarnate state becomes voluntarily subject to certain conditions which were

[1] *Ad Rom.* 6.　　　　　　[2] *Ad Ephes.* 1.

wholly absent till then.   Whatever may be true of the
Apologists we cannot ascribe to Ignatius a Hellenization
of Christianity. We must see in this phraseology the
presupposition that God[1], who is essentially spirit, is
in Himself beyond those experiences which we know of
only in connexion with the life of the world and with
human nature. The contrast spirit-flesh, implied in this
passage, and quite in line with Ignatius' strong opposition to any Docetic explaining away of the reality of the
Incarnation, appears also in the homily to which
Clement's name was attached[2]. If Lightfoot is right,
Clement in his genuine letter spoke, in the same way as
Ignatius, of the sufferings of Christ as the sufferings of
God[3]—"You were satisfied," says Clement, "with the
provision of God, and paying attention to His words
you stored them up carefully in your hearts, and kept
His sufferings before your eyes." At the same time, we
must not interpret the language of Ignatius as though
the later discrimination in connexion with Christology,
which appears with the formulation of the doctrine of
the Two Natures, and is applied in such a document as
the *Tome* of Leo, were already present. The most
striking dogmatic passage in Ignatius, *ad Ephes.* vii, 2,
points forward to that formulation, but is too rhetorical

[1] Whether Ignatius does or does not ever speak of Jesus
Christ absolutely as God (both Harnack, *Hist. Dogm.* i, p. 189,
and Lightfoot on the passages *ad Trall.* vii, 1, *ad Smyr.* vi, 1,
x, 1, doubt it) he had no hesitation in speaking of Christ as
"our God" (*ad Ephes.* inscription), and using similar phrases.

[2] 2 *Clem.* ix, 5; cf. also xiv.

[3] 1 *Clem.* ii, 1. Lightfoot's arguments for θεοῦ not χριστοῦ
being the original reading after ἐφοδίοις are powerful.

to be construed as exact theology. There also we have
an antithesis "first passible and then impassible" which,
when taken with the words already quoted from the
letter to Polycarp, gives us the notion of passibility as
a temporal circumstance attaching to the revelation of
Christ our God in the flesh or in man, but possessing no
eternal grounding in the divine nature[1].

The language of Ignatius reappears in one of the few
fragments which remain to us from the extensive work
of Melito of Sardis. Anastasius Sinaita, a Greek ecclesi-
astic of the seventh century, has preserved for us words
used by Melito in the course of a sermon on the Passion.
"God," he says, "suffered at the hand of Israel[2]."
But the extract which Anastasius quoted from the third
book of the work on the Incarnation of Christ, written
against Marcion, shows that Melito was a much more
considerable theologian than Ignatius. He distinguishes
with great clearness between the Godhead and the manhood in Christ, remarks on the obvious reality of His
soul and body in respect of His human nature which
was like to ours[3], and declares that "He, the self-same
person being God and at the same time also perfect man,
gave us a pledge of His two substances (οὐσίας)"; it is
natural to conclude from the general character of the

[1] The whole passage runs: "There is one physician, both
fleshly and spiritual, begotten and unbegotten, God in man,
true life in death, both of Mary and of God, first passible and
then impassible, Jesus Christ our Lord."

[2] Routh, *Rel. Sacr.* I, p. 122.

[3] The words in Greek (in Routh, I, p. 121) are τὸ ἀληθὲς
καὶ ἀφάνταστον τῆς ψυχῆς αὐτοῦ καὶ τοῦ σώματος τῆς καθ᾽
ἡμᾶς ἀνθρωπίνης φύσεως. The soul must be the human soul.

fragment that Melito referred the suffering to the
human οὐσία, though the oneness of the Person to
which he here draws attention, allows him to speak elsewhere of God as having suffered, precisely as later
theologians were prepared to do, not in such rhetorical
phrases as we shall find in Tertullian, but in considered
dogmatic statements which were rendered possible by the
doctrine of the *communicatio idiomatum.*

What Loofs calls the "Asia-Minor tradition[1]" in
Christian theology was, by reason of its strong emphasis
upon the Person and work of Christ, the most effective
religious rejoinder to Gnosticism. In so far as the
Gnostics were concerned, as we should believe them to
have been concerned, with religious values, and not
merely intent upon theosophical speculations, the
orthodox tradition had something better to offer. But
more was needed if Christianity was to be vindicated as
the true philosophy of religion against both the Hellenic
schools and the Gnostic sects. This is the special importance of the work of the Apologists. Justin, in
particular, was many-sided. We know how he stated
the Christian case, as he saw it, against the Jews, and the
Apologies show us enough of the line which he took in
contrasting Christian doctrine with Greek philosophy
to enable us to apprehend the mixture of conciliation and
of controversy in his method. Two discourses against the
Greeks are lost, as is the work against all the heresies,
and the work against Marcion. How he opposed the
celestial mythology of the Gnostics and the dualism of
Marcion is sufficiently clear from his conception of God

[1] *Leitfaden*[4], p. 143.

as expressed in the Apologies. From both Plato and the Stoics he had learned much in the way of outlook and general conceptions, and his own statement is that the teachings of Plato are not different from Christ's, while not absolutely similar, as is true also of the Stoics and others[1]. And in his doctrine of God, while he has a firm hold of the divine personality, and several times speaks of God as the Father or Creator of all things, thus treading confidently on ground which the Greek, unlike the Jew and the Christian, always approached with a good deal of hesitation and uncertainty, his assertions of the transcendence, ineffability and immutability of God place him quite in line with the Platonic tendency to define God in such terms of contrast with the world and with man as, when extended to their furthest point, lead to a series of negations and the complete absence of positive descriptions[2]. That God is ἄτρεπτος, unchangeable, is a conviction common to him and to those for whom he writes; what he feels that he needs to expound is the mystery of a second place after the eternal God being given by Christians to the Crucified[3]. It is for him one of the superiorities of

[1] *Apol.* II, 13. 2.
[2] See especially *Apol.* II, 5. 1, where it is said that God has no name: there are only descriptions of Him drawn from His works. The famous words in the *Timaeus,* 28 c, "The father and maker of all this universe is past finding out, and even if we found him, to tell him to all men would be impossible" (Jowett), give precisely the kind of difficulty which the Greek felt and the Jew did not. Plato has, indeed, much that is positive to say about God, but one-sided emphasis on the divine transcendence owes itself in germ to him.
[3] *Apol.* I, 13. 4.

Christian theology that, in contrast with the earthly and
unedifying experiences ascribed to the gods of Greece,
it has nothing to say about God which is incompatible
with His being "unbegotten and impassible[1]." Justin
describes the incarnation of the Word of the unbegotten
and ineffable God as due to His desire to share in our
sufferings and provide healing for them[2]. The question
whether the generation of the Son by the Father involved any ascription of "passion" to the divine nature
is already answered implicitly by Justin in the negative,
long before Arius and Eunomius raised it as a problem for
their opponents to meet, and constructed out of it one
of the main positions of their own theology.

The doctrine of Tatian points in the same direction
as that of Justin, whose disciple he had been. And it is
remarkable that though Tatian has nothing but scorn
for the whole heritage of Greek wisdom, his interest in
the Gospels as a theological source seems almost entirely
non-existent in his *Oratio ad Graecos*. The important
chapters 4 and 5 are more metaphysical than evangelical.
He never speaks of Jesus Christ, never even of the Son of
God, but of the Logos and of the begetting of the Logos.
That God suffered any loss through the generation of
the Son to be the principle of the world is expressly
denied. He is not made defective by the fact that the
Logos came into being (*i.e.* as personally distinct) "by
participation (μερισμόν) not by abscission." Tatian
makes use at this point of a metaphor of the torch and
light kindled from it, which in the more common form
of the sun and the ray became so familiar an illustration

[1] *Apol.* I, 25. 2.　　　　[2] *Apol.* II, 13. 4.

of the relation between the Father and the Son. Yet Tatian in one passage speaks after the manner of Ignatius of the suffering of God; the language indeed is even stronger. The Spirit is described as the "minister of the suffering God[1]." Tatian is one of those to whom the author of the "Little Labyrinth" refers as persons "among whom Christ is spoken of as God (θεολογεῖται ὁ χριστός)"; such as they could not avoid expressions like the above. These all follow from the belief in the Incarnation, that, as Tatian says, "God was born in human form[2]." It would be a mistake to suppose that the subordinationism of the Apologists, and language which suggests that the Logos is a second God, led them to conceive of the Deity of the Logos as essentially other and lower than the Godhead of the Father. "The Apologists," says Harnack, "only know of one kind of divine nature and this is that which belongs to the Logos[3]." If, as he adds a little later[4], "in virtue of his finite origin, it is possible and proper for the Logos to enter into the finite, to act, to speak, and to appear," that involves no notion of the Logos as, in nature, changeable or passible. The Arian doctrine of a created Logos, who is changeable, is not that of these early theologians, even though Tatian can call Him the "first-born work of the Father[5]."

The contrast between the Christian doctrine of one God and the pagan mythology of many gods was a

[1] διάκονος τοῦ πεπονθότος θεοῦ, *Oratio*, 13. The reference is to the Crucifixion, but the participle is used almost adjectivally.

[2] *Oratio*, 21. He never gives a theology of the Incarnation, but pours ridicule on Greek theophanies.

[3] *Hist. Dogm.* II, p. 211 (Eng. tr.).

[4] *Ib.* p. 212.   [5] *Oratio*, 5.

favourite one with Christian apologists. And of that contrast an important element was the comparison between the spiritual nature of the true God and the materiality of the gods depicted by Homer and other poets. Theophilus of Antioch does not spare his correspondent Autolycus in emphasizing the distinction. Like Justin he has something to say about the names which may be given to God, but attaches them to realities in the divine nature, not to works done by God in His activity towards the world. At the same time, the attributes of anger and mercy are ascribed to Him in relation to the varied behaviour of men. God is certainly angry, "for He is angry with the evil-doers, but good and kind and merciful towards them who love and fear Him." When Theophilus goes on almost immediately to say that God is "unchangeable, inasmuch as He is immortal," we must regard him as meaning that no outside force can so act upon God as to alter the essential constancy of His nature. In this sense he could have used of God, as Justin did, the adjective $\dot{\alpha}\pi\alpha\theta\dot{\eta}s$, but the Stoic idea of a God who is above all feeling would be incompatible with what he has already said[1].

Athenagoras in his *Legatio* directly attacks the poetic, especially the Homeric, attribution of emotions to the gods. "Neither anger nor desire nor yearning nor any generative seed is in God." Men are contemptible when they yield to anger and grief: how much more the gods[2]. The

---

[1] *Ad Autol.* i, 3. 4.

[2] *Legat.* 21; cf. Tatian, *Oratio*, 8, on the gods (he calls them demons) from Zeus downwards, being overcome by the same passions as men.

true God, who is an indivisible unity, is also impassible[1]. This is one among a number of negative epithets which Athenagoras uses in order to make clear the divine transcendence[2]. He is careful to show that the Christian belief in the Son of God involves nothing ridiculous, nothing comparable with the fables of the poets. The value to the Apologists of the Logos-doctrine as the means of preserving the pure spirituality of the Godhead in connexion with the notions of Fatherhood and Son-ship is noticeable in the tenth chapter of the *Legatio*. The Son is the Logos of the Father "in conception and actuality," and "from the beginning God, being eternal mind (νοῦς), Himself had in Himself the Logos." Athenagoras comes nearer than does Justin or Tatian to Origen's doctrine of the eternal generation of the Son.

The Gnostic controversy, important for the future in so many ways, was not least so in leading the chief opponents of Gnosticism to build up their doctrines of God and of Christ in sharp opposition to the principal positions of the Gnostic schools. So far as the former was concerned, the tendency of Gnosticism was, by refusing to identify the Supreme God with the Creator, to remove God from direct contact with the world and to emphasize His transcendence. Thus Basilides, as his theology is given by Hippolytus, employed in his account of the Supreme God the negative method in an unsurpassable degree. The "God-who-was-not, whom Aristotle calls

[1] *Legat.* 8.
[2] *Legat.* 10. God is described as unoriginate (ἀγένητος), invisible, impassible, incomprehensible (ἀκατάληπτος) and incapable of circumscription (ἀχώρητος).

Concept of Concept, but (Basilides) Him-who-is-Not, without conception, perception, counsel, choice, passion or desire willed to create a cosmos[1]"—though Hippolytus points out that will was really as absent as conception or perception. A similar, though less negatively described, transcendence belongs to God in the doctrine of Valentinus, as Hippolytus describes it: "the Father was alone, unbegotten, having neither place, nor time, nor counsellor, nor any other thing that by any other figure of speech could be understood as essence[2]." At the same time, Valentinus rises to a much higher conception of the nature of God, by the use of language which recalls St John, though Hippolytus may have connected it, in the Gnostic leader's case, with Pythagoras and the *Timaeus* of Plato. "God was all love and love is not love unless there be something to be loved." Hence it happened that the Father, not loving to be alone, "projected and engendered" the first two aeons Mind and Truth, and so the movement towards the formation of the Pleroma began. Then later, through the action of the youngest aeon, Sophia, who foolishly tried to imitate the Father, the first step towards the origination of a lower world was taken. To the Father alone belonged the power of producing by Himself a substance with form and shape. Through Sophia's act the spiritual harmony of the Pleroma was destroyed; suffering entered it in the grief of Sophia over the abortion ($\H{\epsilon}\kappa\tau\rho\omega\mu\alpha$) brought forth by her[3]. Valentinus went on to show how, even when the formless offspring

---

[1] *Philosoph.* VII, 21 (Legge's translation).
[2] *Ibid.* VI, 29.   [3] *Ibid.* 30–1.

had been transformed by the work of the aeons Christ
and the Holy Spirit into "Sophia without the Pleroma,"
passion still remained while she sought after the aeon
Christ who had returned to His place within the Pleroma.
So Jesus, "the common fruit" of the aeons, was sent
forth to be her husband and to relieve her of the passions
of fear, grief, perplexity and supplication to which she
was subject. The passions themselves He transformed
into "underlying beings" ($\dot{\upsilon}\pi o\sigma\tau\acute{a}\tau o\upsilon\varsigma$ $o\dot{\upsilon}\sigma\acute{\iota}a\varsigma$), connected respectively with the soul, matter, the demons,
and the way of repentance[1].

Thus did Valentinus explain the beginnings of change
and passion and attached them to events in the transcendental world. He regarded the Father, to whom he
gave the name of Abyss ($\beta\upsilon\theta\acute{o}\varsigma$), as unaffected by these
events. But Irenaeus in his criticism tried to show that
the supreme God of the Valentinian system was Himself
involved in the failure and error which had found their
way into the Pleroma. "That light of the Father of
which they speak will be subject to the reproach of not
being able to enlighten and fill all that falls within it. So,
speaking of those things as the fruit of defect, and the
work of error, they will bring defect and error within
the Pleroma and into the bosom of the Father[2]." The
charges brought by the Valentinians against the
Demiurge, in connexion with the material and temporal creation, fall back upon the Father. If the Father
did not allow or approve such creation, then the Demiurge was stronger than He; if He allowed, but did not

[1] *Philosoph.* vi, 32.
[2] *Cont. haer.* ii, 3. 4 in Harvey's edition.

approve, "he either, though able to prevent it, allowed
it because of some necessity, or he was not able. But if
he was not able, he is without strength and weak; but if
he was able, he was a deceiver and hypocrite and the
slave of necessity, not consenting and yet making con-
cessions as though he did consent. And allowing in the
beginning that error to be established and to grow, in
later times he tried to destroy it, when now many had
evilly perished because of the defect[1]."

---

[1] *Cont. haer.* II, 4. 3. Irenaeus returns to the whole question
in II, 21–7. He argues that if the aeons are born of the Father,
"of the same substance as He, and like to their Father," then
the result must be that "they will remain impassible even as
He is impassible who generated them" (21. 3); "if they are
kindled as lights from light, the Aeons from Logos, and Logos
from Nous, and Nous from Bythus, as, we may say, torches
from a torch; then in respect of birth and greatness perhaps
they will differ from one another; but since they are of the
same substance as the Cause of their generation, either they
will all remain impassible, or their Father also will share in
their passions" (21. 4). "Whence," he asks, "does passion
arise in the case of that younger Aeon, if the Father's light is
that from which all lights are formed, that light which is by
nature impassible?" (22. 1); as there is no distinction in substance, all alike must be "by nature impassible and unchangeable, or all, along with the Father's light, are passible and open
to the changes of corruption...if it is impious to attribute to
the Father of all ignorance and passion, how do they say that
an Aeon generated by him is passible?" (*ibid.*). Irenaeus,
refusing to distinguish, as the Valentinians did, between the
Father and Nous, and further identifying Nous and Logos,
rules out all possibility of ignorance or suffering being ascribed
to the Logos (22. 2); similarly, it was absurd to predicate
ignorance and passion of Sophia, "let them either abandon
that title for her (*i.e.* Sophia), or cease to speak of her passions.

Irenaeus considered that the logic of the Valentinian position involved the doctrine of a finite and changeable God[1]. He himself asserts in many ways the divine transcendence. God "needs nothing and is self-sufficient[2]": He is "perfect in all ways, equal and like to Himself, wholly light, wholly mind, wholly substance[3]," "rich in all things[4]"; the importance which Irenaeus attaches to revelation is a combination of his beliefs in the transcendence and in the goodness of God. As transcendent He is far beyond human knowledge. His

And let them not say that the whole fullness is spiritual, if this Aeon, though the subject of such mighty passions, dwelt therein; for, not to speak of spiritual substance, not even the soul, if it be brave, will have such experiences" (23. 1). The whole treatment of passion in the spiritual world seemed to Irenaeus to be due to, and vitiated by, an illegitimate anthropomorphic tendency. When the Valentinians talked about "fear and terror and passion and dissolution and the like," they were influenced by conceptions drawn from human behaviour, not from such as were appropriate in relation to "spiritual and divine substance" (25. 1). With Irenaeus' argument, that the admission of passion, in the Aeon of Sophia, into the transcendental world, leads logically to the doctrine of a passible God, may be compared the arraignment by Clement of Alexandria of the Oriental school of Valentinians in the person of Theodotus for impiety in saying that God had suffered, a deduction which Clement draws from what Theodotus had said concerning the "sympathy" of the Father in making Himself intelligible to Sige, "for sympathy is the suffering of one on account of the suffering of another" (*Excerpt. Theod.* 30).

[1] See F. R. M. Hitchcock's note in *Early Church Classics*, "The Treatise of Irenaeus of Lugdunum against the Heresies," vol. I, p. 47.

[2] *Cont. haer.* III, 8. 3.   [3] *Ibid.* IV, 21. 2.   [4] *Ibid.* V, 33. 4.

nature is above all possibility of measurement or com-
prehension[1]; man cannot serve Him so as to add anything to Him[2]. And apart from God, God cannot be
known[3]. But the desire and purpose of self-revelation
belongs to the nature of God. Irenaeus indeed finds this
principle eternally existent in God, and his doctrine of
the Trinity is closely connected with it, though it is a
false antithesis when Harnack contrasts the idea of an
essential Trinity and a Trinity of revelation, and attributes only the latter to Irenaeus[4]. The relation of the
Divine Persons in the Godhead is not for Irenaeus
dependent upon the need and desire of God for self-
revelation to that which lies outside the Godhead. When
he says "the Father is the invisible of the Son, and the
Son is the visible of the Father[5]," he is thinking of the
revelation of the unseen Father through the Word made
visible at the Incarnation; but his earlier quotation
from an unnamed author that "the unmeasured Father
is measured in the Son; for the Son is the measure of the
Father, seeing that He contains Him[6]" suggests a
relationship which eternally exists between the Divine
Persons, and is in no way contingent. At the same time,
the metaphor, several times used by Irenaeus, of the
Son and the Spirit as the "hands" of the Father[7],

---

[1] *Cont. haer.* IV, 33. 1.   [2] *Ibid.* IV, 25. 1.

[3] "Sine Deo non cognosci Deum," *Ibid.* IV, 11. 3.

[4] *Hist. Dogm.* II, p. 265, "his (*i.e.* Irenaeus') statement
that the Logos has revealed the Father from the beginning
shows that this relationship is always within the sphere of
revelation. The Son then exists because He gives a revelation."

[5] *Cont. haer.* IV, 11. 4.   [6] *Ibid.* IV, 6.

[7] *Ibid.* IV, 34. 1; V, 6. 1 and elsewhere.

through which He creates, is reminiscent of the Apologists' notion of the Logos as the cosmological principle, the medium of creation.

Whenever thought of that kind appears, something of finitude, owing to His capacity for entering into relations with the finite, may be regarded as conceivable in the case of the Logos. But Irenaeus never laid any stress upon this, and spoke quite clearly of the impassibility of the Word. In the Incarnation "the invisible was made visible, and the incomprehensible comprehensible, and the impassible passible[1]." As against the Gnostics, with their alternative theories of a merely apparent humanity in Christ and a distinction between the Jesus who underwent the passion and the Christ who remained untouched thereby[2], Irenaeus emphasizes the unity of the Person of the Incarnate Christ and the reality of the sufferings, in expressions that would hardly have been regarded as orthodox after the Patripassian and the Monophysite controversies[3]. On the other hand, when he is opposing opinions of an Ebionite character and those who said that Jesus Christ was only a man, he sharply discriminates between the human and the divine elements in the Incarnation. "How," he asks, "could we be united to incorruption and immortality, unless

---

[1] *Cont. haer.* III, 17. 6.   [2] *Ibid.* III, 18. 3.
[3] *E.g.* "Commixtio et communio Dei et hominis," *Ibid.* IV, 34. 4; cf. III, 19. 5 "Solus vere magister Dominus noster, et bonus vere Filius Dei et patiens, Verbum Dei Patris Filius Hominis factus." Harnack, *Hist. Dogm.* II, p. 276, says that besides the dogma of God the Creator, cardinal for Irenaeus is the doctrine of Jesus Christ as "one and the same person, who created the world, was born, suffered and ascended."

first of all incorruption and immortality had been made that which we are, that the corruptible might be absorbed by incorruption, and the mortal by immortality, that we might receive the adoption of sons[1]?" The word "absorbed" might be understood as implying such a taking up of the human into the divine that the characteristics of the humanity were lost in the Godhead; but in his continuation of the argument Irenaeus speaks in a way which suggests a wide separation within the sphere of the Incarnation. Christ was man, uncomely and passible and also the holy Lord, Wonderful, Counsellor, Mighty God. "He was Man that He might be tempted, so also He was the Word that He might be glorified; the Word indeed was quiescent in the temptation and crucifixion and death, but assisted the humanity in the victory and endurance and benevolence and resurrection and assumption[2]." The latter distinctions— Christ was born, suffered, etc. not in His divine but in His human nature—are already present in this passage.

Irenaeus' characteristic doctrine of redemption, while expressed in a manner which implies the readiness of the Logos, out of love for man, to enter into the conditions of human life and subject Himself to its experiences, to "become what we are in order to make us to be what He is Himself[3]," involves no idea of any essential capacity for suffering in the Logos. On the contrary, the thought of the Incarnation and of the "recapitula-

---

[1] *Cont. haer.* III, 20. I.

[2] *Ibid.* III, 20. 3. The text follows the Greek as given by Theodoret, *Dial.* III.

[3] *Cont. haer.* v, *praef.*

tion " by the Son of Man of the long roll of humanity, so that men might recover in Him that state of existence after the image and likeness of God, which they had lost in Adam[1], assumes that through the redemptive work of the Word mankind regains a perfection which was his at the beginning, and in which state he was free from suffering and death. The fruit of the incarnation of the Word is the deification of man. It was for this end that the Word was "united with His own creation, and made a passible man[2]." Even if we take that other strain in Irenaeus' anthropology which leads him to conceive of man as not originally perfect but only capable of perfection[3], man's destiny is still represented as a participation in the essentially divine attributes of immortality and incorruption. "The sole way," says Harnack, "in which immortality as a physical condition can be obtained is by its possessor uniting himself *realiter* with human nature, in order to deify it 'by adoption' ('per adoptionem'), such is the technical term of Irenaeus[4]."

It never occurred to Irenaeus to look for any archetype of human passibility in the divine nature. That was in itself beyond all experiences that we can connect with suffering. And when, as he often did, he thought teleologically, he saw the divine grace working for the assimilation of human nature to the divine by freeing it from those limitations and defects which held it back

---

[1] *Cont. haer.* III, 19. I.   [2] *Ibid.*

[3] As in IV, 62, where we have the paradox—God could give man perfection from the beginning, but man could not receive it, for he was a babe; the reference is to I Cor. iii, 2. Hence human progress must be gradual.

[4] *Hist. Dogm.* II, 241.

from its true end. In one passage[1] Irenaeus gives a
very full statement of man's onward progress towards
proximity to the uncreated God. His destiny is to see
God; "now the vision of God effects incorruption, and
incorruption makes man near to God."

There is a richness of conception and power of
synthesis in Irenaeus which raises him above the
Apologists, though he was not a deep philosophical
thinker, as passages in the *Legatio* suggest to have been
true of Athenagoras. In his theology God seems less
aloof in His transcendence. Morally and spiritually He
is portrayed as more akin to man. The Incarnation
effects the closest union of Him with man. But that
impassibility is for him an essential attribute of the
divine nature, we cannot doubt.

We have seen that Irenaeus charged Valentinus with
giving such an account of the beginnings of intellectual
and moral confusion and error in the spiritual world as
logically to implicate the Supreme God in responsibility,
and so to make Him less than perfect. The argument is
not convincing, or rather it proves too much, for if it
could be argued that the unbegotten Father of the
Valentinian theosophy was shown to be imperfect in
power or in goodness by reason of the fall—for so we
may call it—of Sophia, and of the resulting consequences, any doctrine of God which asserted His
creative activity, and to that extent brought Him into
touch with a world in which error and sin had a place,
would be open to a similar charge. In point of fact, the
religious interest of the Valentinian system lies not in

[1] *Cont. haer.* iv, 63. 2.

the transcendental mythology of the origin of error and sin, of the passions and of the material world, but in the redemption whereby creation was brought back into harmony with the Supreme God. This redemption meant at each stage of its progress a purification of those passions which first within the Pleroma and then outside it were the cause of the alienation of created existences from the perfect Father. Hippolytus has given us a summary statement of the different steps in the soterio-logy. After showing how the psychic and ignorant Demiurge was said to be corrected of his foolishness by the teaching of Sophia without, he goes on to say: "It was necessary, then, that the things on high having been put straight, in the same sequence correction should come to those here, as the Christ, who on high was projected by Nous and Aletheia, put straight the passions of Sophia without, that is of the Ectroma. And again the Saviour who was born through Mary came to set straight the passions of the soul[1]."

The connexion between the spiritual and the im-passible is clear in the Valentinian Christology. Into its complications we need not go, but in respect of two of the four elements of which Christ the Saviour was composed, He was incapable of suffering. Not only did the pre-existent Saviour, who descended at the baptism, remain impassible, "for it was not possible that He should suffer since He was incomprehensible and invisible,... but they say that not even that seed which was from His mother[2] suffered, for that also is impassible inasmuch as

[1] *Philosoph.* vi, 36, tr. Legge.
[2] The Lower Sophia or Achamoth.

it is spiritual and invisible also to the Demiurge himself."
He who suffered was the psychical Christ (the psychical
element being received from the Demiurge), with that
body which was made in an ineffable manner[1]. The
distinction between the spiritual and the psychical was
of great importance in this system, reappearing also
when the question arises of those who shall be saved.
The spiritual seed was the principle of union between
the higher sphere of reality and those men who were
either assured of or capable of salvation. In this doctrine
there was implicit a contrast between bodily passions and
spiritual passionlessness. How far the sharp dichotomy
between spirit and matter, relieved only by the middle
term of the psychic element, worked itself out in ethical
antinomianism is a question difficult to answer with
assurance. The *Letter of Ptolemaeus to Flora* suggests
nothing of the kind, and though Hippolytus ascribes
immoral teaching to the Valentinian teacher Marcus, of
whose licentiousness in conduct Irenaeus had had a good
deal to say, he does not involve Valentinus himself in any
similar charges[2]. But the account which Irenaeus gives
of the claims made and the practices indulged in by the
Valentinians elect seems to be based on real knowledge
of the teaching of a section, at least, of the Valentinian
school[3].

[1] Iren. *c. haer.* I, 1. 13.
[2] VI, 42. Marcus "ruined many (Legge's tr. of ἐξαφανίσας
which has the idea of intellectual rather than of moral destruction), and led many of them to become his disciples (by)
teaching them to be indifferent to sin"; cf. Iren. I, 7.
[3] Iren. I, 1. 12. There was probably some such catch-
phrase, as Irenaeus mentions, τὰ σαρκικὰ τοῖς σαρκικοῖς, τὰ

But whatever inconsistencies, and consequences incompatible with belief in the supreme transcendental God, orthodox antagonists could point to in the Gnostic systems, there can be no doubt that the leading Gnostic teachers, Saturninus, Carpocrates, Basilides, Valentinus, and Marcion, who may be classed with the others in this connexion, founded their elaborate doctrines on belief in a God to whom nothing of the nature of passion could be attributed, a God quite exempt from those limitations which were involved in their conceptions of the Demiurge. In this fundamental notion the Gnostics and their opponents were not at variance; only the Gnostics were unable to combine their idea of the transcendence of God with the idea of His creatorship of the material world. Nor is their teleology, allowing for the distinctive doctrines concerning human salvation which were taught in the Gnostic schools, essentially different from such an ideal as at the end of his great work Hippolytus puts before his readers. There he points the way to salvation through the knowledge of "the God Who Is." To the man thus instructed he says: "Thou shalt speak with God and be joint-heir with Christ, not enslaved by desires, nor sufferings, nor diseases. For thou (wilt) have become God[1]. For whatever sufferings thou underwent as man, thou hast shown that thou art a man; but whatever is appurtenant to a God, that God has promised to bestow, because thou hast been made divine, since thou hast been begotten immortal[2]."

πνευματικὰ τοῖς πνευματικοῖς, dangerous in itself and capable of grave abuse.　　　　[1] In the Greek, γέγονας γὰρ Θεός.
[2] *Philosoph.* x, 34. (Legge.)

The controversy with the Gnostics was within the field of the philosophy of religion. The curiosities of the mythological expression of the Gnostic schemes are but the external, imaginative setting of ideas which revolved round the problems of creation, evil, and redemption. With its consequences for the Church we are not here concerned, except in so far as it led, both in the Rule of Faith, and in the writings of the theologians, to a deliberate emphasis upon the fact that the Creator of the world was the true God, whose spiritual nature was in no way compromised by His direct responsibility for the existence of the world, and also upon the unity of the Person of Jesus Christ, the reality of His human nature and of His sufferings. The theology of Irenaeus is the true successor to the passionate declarations of Ignatius.

2. THE MODALIST CONTROVERSY AND WESTERN THEOLOGY

But the successful opposition to the Gnostic schools which, whatever influence they had in promoting a "Hellenization" of Christianity more moderate than their own, were quite unable to find a permanent place within the Church, did not prevent the raising, specifically within the field of dogmatics, of questions affecting the interpretation of the Rule of Faith with regard to God and to Christ. And the form in which these questions were raised in what is known as Modalistic Monarchianism, and the answers given by the exponents of this type of doctrine, brought into prominence the notion of the suffering of God and compelled a formal consideration of the problems which the language of earlier writers implicitly contained. Obviously, if God had been so wholly present in Jesus Christ that, during the Incarnation, God was Jesus and was not to be found anywhere else, the belief in a divine, impassible nature could no longer be retained. Only a Docetic doctrine could have given a way out, and any such road would have led right away from the religious interests of the Modalists.

Of all the Modalist teachers, the most crudely Patripassian of whom we have any knowledge was Noetus, who taught in Asia Minor and later at Rome, where he founded a school. Hippolytus reports him as teaching that "the Father and the Son so-called are one and the same.... One was He who appeared and underwent birth from a Virgin and dwelt as a man among men.... He also suffered, being nailed to the Tree, and gave up His Spirit to Himself, and died and did not die[1]." The complete immersion of God in finite experiences is here expounded definitely enough, but it is necessary to remember, as Harnack has pointed out, that what interested the Modalists—and he would extend this to all Monarchians—was not philosophical theology but the history of salvation[2]. Noetus and his school were anxious to assert as emphatically as possible the full Deity of Jesus Christ, and they saw no other way of doing that

[1] *Philosoph.* IX, 10; cf. x, 27: "The Father and God of the universals is passionless and immortal when He does not suffer and die, but when (the) Passion comes, He suffers and dies." Cf. in the tractate *contra Noetum* Hippolytus' summary description, "he said that Christ was the Father, and that the Father Himself was born and suffered."

[2] *Hist. Dogm.* III, p. 64.

than by distinguishing Fatherhood and Sonship in the one God only as the invisible and the manifested. This they maintained without compromise, but thereby they made it clear that the element of passibility in the divine nature was wholly dependent upon God's free resolve to enter the world for the salvation of men. The distinction between the invisible and the manifested, which Noetus' doctrine declared, was carried further by his contemporary Praxeas, for first-hand knowledge of whom we are dependent upon Tertullian's treatise against him. From the opening pages we should gather that Praxeas was no more subtle than Noetus, teaching that "the Father Himself descended into the Virgin, Himself was born of her, Himself died, in short that He Himself was Jesus Christ": hence Tertullian found ground for his famous saying that at Rome Praxeas "crucified the Father[1]." But Praxeas and his followers tried to make distinctions within the sphere of the Incarnation. There they discriminated between Father and Son, saying that "the Son is flesh, that is man, that is Jesus, but the Father spirit, that is God, that is Christ." Tertullian made full controversial use of this admission, even suggesting that they had picked up this curious kind of "monarchy," which led to a distinction between Jesus and Christ, from the Valentinian school[2]. What we should infer is that, with whatever inconsistency, these Modalists shrank from such Patripassian statements as would imply that in the Person of Christ the divine in itself, *simpliciter*, was the subject of the finite experiences and the suffering.

Yet further reservations appear in the formulae of the

---

[1] *Adv. Prax.* 1.   [2] *Ibid.* 27.

two Roman Bishops of the early third century to whom Hippolytus is so uncomplimentary. Neither Zephyrinus nor Callistus was an expert theologian, and the position at Rome was far from easy. The younger Theodotus and his school of learned critics were interpreting the divinity of Jesus as a moral assimilation to God[1]; Noetus' successors, Epigonus and Cleomenes and, most dangerous of all, the Egyptian Sabellius, were at the other extreme, emphasizing the essential divinity of Jesus in such a way as to rule out any doctrine of the Trinity which asserted pre-temporal relationships of a personal character within the Godhead, while Hippolytus, the one really well-equipped theologian of the Western Church, was giving to the Logos-doctrine a scientific expression which was not free from the defects of the theology of the Apologists and raised doubts as to its fidelity to monotheism[2]. Zephyrinus may have been "an ignorant and unlettered man," and the statements of his which Hippolytus quotes are, when taken together, unsatisfactory and confused, but they suggest that he wanted to express his belief that He who was born and crucified was truly God, without identifying Him with the Father or saying that the Father had suffered. "I know," he declared, "one God, Christ Jesus, and beside Him I know no other, begotten and susceptible of suffering"; but he also said "The Father did not die, but the Son[3]." If Hippolytus gives us at all

[1] Cf. Euseb. *Eccl. Hist.* v, 28.
[2] In *Philosoph.* ix, 11 it is implied that Callistus had popular sympathy on his side when he accused Hippolytus of ditheism.
[3] *Philosoph.* ix, 11.

an accurate account of the opinions of Callistus we can see in them the workings of a mind which, at least, understood the needs and the difficulties of scientific theology. It was after his excommunication of Sabellius that Callistus put out what Hippolytus calls his heresy, but what he certainly intended as a comprehensive formula in which all the opposed factions could find something to please them[1]. His own theology, especially as regards the Trinity, presents difficulties into which we need not enter; what is immediately relevant is his way of avoiding Patripassian language. Having distinguished between "that which is seen, which is man," which is "the Son," and "the spirit contained in the Son," which is "the Father," and repudiated any doctrine of two Gods, he seems, after the statement about the deification of the flesh, to have concluded his teaching with the words, "this Person (πρόσωπον, that is, the one God) cannot be two, and so the Father suffered with the Son." This terminology, says Hippolytus, was due to his unwillingness to say that the Father had suffered and was one Person[2]. In other words, the suffering of the Son could not leave the Father unaffected because of the unity between the Father and the Son which was involved in the belief in

[1] Even the Theodotians would recognize something of their own doctrine in the words "for the Father who was in Him, having taken on Him the flesh, deified it by uniting it to Himself, and made it one (ἕν)—so that Father and Son are called one God" (Legge: "so that He is called Father and Son, one God").

[2] *Philosoph.* ix, 12. I.e. he wished to avoid saying that there was no distinction between the Father and the Son.

One God; on the other hand, the Father was not the Son, and the Son was the immediate experient of the sufferings. We have exactly the same formula referred to by Tertullian in the *Adversus Praxeam*, with the same comment that it was intended as an escape from "blasphemy" against the Father. Tertullian will not let it pass. "The Father," he says, "did not suffer with the Son.... What is compassion but suffering with another? If the Father is impassible, then He cannot suffer with another; if He can suffer with another, then He is passible.... You fear to speak of Him as passible, whom you speak of as suffering with another. But the Father is as unable to suffer with another as the Son is unable to suffer in virtue of His divinity.... What the Spirit of God can suffer in the Son the Father could not be regarded as suffering, since the Spirit suffered not in the Father, but in the Son. But it is clear that the Spirit of God suffered nothing in His own name, since whatever He suffered He suffered in the Son. Quite different was the idea of the Father suffering with the Son in the flesh." The "suffering" of the Spirit Tertullian explains, by comparison with what is true in believers, as being the assistance which the Spirit gives in suffering, "He does not suffer, but gives the power to suffer[1]." A new and more philosophical turn was given to Modalism by Sabellius, whose teaching, delivered chiefly in the school he founded at Rome, became the object of peculiar detestation in the East for over a century. He gave a much more subtle interpretation than Noetus had done to a doctrine of the unity of the Godhead which

[1] *Adv. Prax.* 29.

M

allowed of no essential distinction of Persons. But Harnack is right in saying that the attempt Sabellius made "to demonstrate the succession of the Prosopa" is out of line with formulas asserting the suffering of the Father with the Son and "may be regarded as a return to the strict form of Modalism[1]." Methodius brings against him the charge of teaching that "the Almighty has suffered[2]," and this is a logical deduction inasmuch as in the Sabellian doctrine God is extended ($\pi\lambda\alpha\tau\acute{v}\nu\epsilon\tau\alpha\iota$) from being first of all Father into later existences as Son and as Holy Spirit[3]. On the one hand, there are elements in Sabellianism to which Dorner in his great work on the Doctrine of the Person of Christ devotes much attention, which point to a conclusion other than that he held the whole of God to be present in each particular manifestation and explain how it comes about that Epiphanius can acquit him of Patripassianism[4]. As an instance may be given the account of Sabellius' teaching in the *Expositio Fidei* attributed to Gregory Thaumaturgus. It is true that the writer ascribes to Sabellius the identification of the Father with the Son; but his continuation alters the appearance of the doctrine— "he says that the Father is He who speaks, and the Son the Word abiding in the Father and manifested at the season of the creation; then, after the fulfilment of all things, He returns to God; the same is his teaching concerning the Spirit[5]." In estimating the character of the

[1] *Hist. Dogm.* iii, pp. 86 f.
[2] *Sympos.* viii, 10.
[3] Ath. *Or. C. Arianos*, iv, 25.   [4] *Haer.* 62.
[5] Quoted by Dorner, Div. i, vol. ii, p. 476 of the English translation.

Modalist conception of the passibility of God, it is
necessary to lay due stress on the passibility being the
result of the action of the divine Will, whereby God
condescends to limit Himself in such ways as will enable
Him to enter upon the level of finite existence through
the Incarnation. It is not that in itself the divine nature
is capable of suffering. Dorner does, indeed, argue for a
notion of this kind in the doctrine of Praxeas in connexion with his teaching as to the self-identification of
the Father with the flesh which He assumed, "so that
He really became man; and 'caro' with all its liability
to suffering is, not something foreign to Him, but a
momentum of Himself. This incorporation of humanity
with His substance evidently presupposes, however, that
the Father was in one aspect susceptible to the finite, to
the passible; and it is this aspect which is manifested in
the Incarnation[1]." But this is to read between the lines
of Tertullian's attack upon Praxeas with much more
assurance than seems justified by what Tertullian
actually says. And when Tertullian is concerned to
confute the idea that in the Person of Christ any mixture of substances, of flesh and spirit, has taken place,
Dorner ascribes such a doctrine not to Praxeas but to
Tertullian's construction of the results of what Praxeas
taught, and even these as logical results rather than as
actual tenets[2]. Accordingly it is going much too far to
speak of this form of Patripassianism as possessing the
"ethnic appearance of rendering God's $\phi\acute{\upsilon}\sigma\iota\varsigma$ immediately finite[3]," and there is no good reason to

[1] Dorner, Div. i, vol. ii, p. 23.   [2] *Ibid.* Note 9, p. 439.
[3] *Ibid.* p. 27.

suppose that Praxeas would have found any fault with
that constant reference to the divine will which Dorner
quotes from the *Compendium Haereticarum Fabularum*
of Theodoret as giving us the view of Noetus, ending
with the words "impassible and immortal, and again
passible and mortal; for being impassible, he says, He
endured of His own will the passion of the cross[1]."
Dorner is right in saying that for Noetus God's "essence
cannot be a check on His will, but remains subject
thereto, and on that account can be made passible,
mortal, and so forth[2]." Whether this be a satisfactory
position or not, it clearly involves no conditions of a
finite or passible character in the divine nature in itself.
That God can put Himself into relations with the world
which render His nature the subject of various events
which take place wholly within the finite order is, with
whatever distinctions among the exponents of this idea,
the common doctrine of all the Modalists. But as a
doctrine it belongs to the dogmatics of the Trinity and
the Incarnation, though as a heresy which was condemned because of its failure to preserve necessary
elements in those dogmatics. It is not an attempt to
bring Christian doctrine into relation with an *a priori*
view that passibility belongs to the divine nature.

Tertullian has come before us as the antagonist of
Patripassianism. The ascription by Praxeas and his
followers of all sorts of finite experiences to the eternal
God seemed to him the height of blasphemy. But it is
interesting to note that his own Trinitarian doctrine
allows, as the Modalist doctrine did not, for the intro-

[1] Dorner, pp. 27 f.   [2] *Ibid.*

duction of a certain natural orientation towards finitude
and passibility into the Godhead. This is due to the
distinctions which he made between the Father and the
Son. But before we come to that, notice may be taken
of a passage in the argument against Marcion, in which
Tertullian throws light on his conception of the
relation of the unchangeableness of the divine nature to
God's possession of feelings such as men experience. One
of the salient points in Marcion's teaching was that the
good God did not act as judge. Tertullian attacks this
denial, asserts that God cares for what happens in
the world—a view essential to belief in God's judgments, and repudiates the anthropomorphism involved
in the contention that if God experiences anger,
jealousy and other feelings He will also have to experience corruption and death. That God did die and
is alive for ever is indeed a glory of Christian belief, but
that has nothing to do with the result of passions which
in the case of men are attached to a condition of corruption. Distinctions must be made between divine and
human nature in respect of feelings, just as the use of
language which speaks of the eyes and feet of God does
not mean than we can compare God with man in this
respect. The divine nature (*substantia*) is free from all
that is corruptible, and the divine feelings will have the
same character. In God everything is divine, not
human, and whereas man, as made in God's image,
possesses in his mind the same feelings as does God, yet
they are not of like quality, "for their conditions and
results differ in accordance with the difference of the
natures." And, Tertullian argues, what is true of

feelings and qualities which the Marcionites deny to God is equally true of such feelings as gentleness and mercy and goodness, "the very womb of them all," which are attributed to Him. In God there is perfection of every feeling. We cannot experience happily the feelings of anger and exasperation, for "God alone is happy in view of His incorruptible nature." That nature is not affected by the feelings which He has, occasioned as they are by the various differing deserts of good and bad men: "and all these He experiences in His own way, in which it is fitting that He should experience them[1]."

The philosophy which most influenced Tertullian was the Stoic. It influenced him sufficiently to lead him to the confident assertion that while God is spirit, He is body as well[2]. And in this passage of his work against Marcion, there is something of the Stoic as well as of the Christian. According to the moral philosophy of the Porch the ethical ideal which is realized in God, and may also be realized in the wise man, involves so complete a control of the passions that the perfect balance of the moral nature is not subject to any disturbance from the emotions. Tertullian's description of the character of the divine feelings reads like a Christianized version of the Stoic exaltation of ἀπάθεια. It was impossible for him to ignore the fact—indeed, as against Marcion, it was necessary to insist—that Scripture attributed to God feelings of different kinds. But these feelings could be accounted for, without affirming any such mutability as would be contrary to the purity and the perfection of the divine nature, by the notion of them as the varying

[1] *Adv. Marc.* II, 16.   [2] *Adv. Prax.* 7.

expressions of God's moral energy in its outgoing towards man.

The Stoics had no difficulty in framing conceptions as to the relation of God to the world, since for them God was the soul of the world, the active force ever moulding the passive material, and in every smallest fragment of the world's being God was present. The world perished and was evolved again in a never-ending series by being absorbed into the vital heat which was identical with God and reconstructed by the divine "rational seeds[1]." Both the consequences and the presuppositions of such extreme immanentism were impossible for any Christian theologian, even though, like Tertullian, he refused the distinction of matter from pure spirit as a true account of the difference between the world and God. Tertullian found all that he needed in what seemed to him to be deducible from the Trinitarian theology. By the distinction of the Persons of the Father and the Son, as he interpreted it, he both, to his own satisfaction, preserved the full truth of the transcendence of God, and also showed how, without diminishing anything of that transcendence, such a contact between God and the world was possible as allowed him the use of such language as "the Son of God was crucified...the Son of God died[2]," which seemed paradoxical just because it assigned to a Person truly divine the experience of finitude and passibility. There are chapters in the treatise against Praxeas which are of great importance as making his position clear. Man

[1] Ueberweg, *History of Philosophy*, I, p. 195 (Eng. tr.).
[2] *De Carne Christi*, 5.

cannot see God's face and live, and yet many see God and live, and that before the Incarnation. The idea that the Old Testament theophanies were manifestations of the Son was well-established before the time of Tertullian[1], but Tertullian's treatment of it is bound up with his theology in the clearest way. The Father is invisible "in view of the fullness of His majesty, the Son visible in view of the measure of His derivation[2]." We must agree that "He was always seen from the beginning who has been seen at the end and that He was not seen at the end, who was not seen from the beginning, and so there are two, seen and unseen[3]." All that is said in the Old Testament concerning the divine theophanies, the walking in the garden, the resting under the oak, and so forth, "ought not to be believed of the Son, unless it had been written, and perhaps ought not to be believed of the Father even if it had been written." So he exposes the error of his opponents, "for being ignorant of the evolution of the whole order of the divine economy through the Son from the beginning, they believe that the Father Himself was both seen and walked with men and worked and suffered thirst and hunger (though the prophet says the Eternal God shall not thirst nor hunger at all: how much more then shall He neither die nor be buried), and so that the one God, that is the Father, always did those things which were accomplished through the Son[4]." A similar argument, adapted to the needs of the polemic against Marcion, is used elsewhere.

---

[1] Cf. Justin, *Dial. cum Tryph.* 56–60; Theophilus, *Ad Autolycum*, II, 22.
[2] *Adv. Prax.* 14.   [3] *Ibid.* 15.   [4] *Ibid.* 16.

Marcion had argued that the Old Testament ascribed to God what was unworthy of the true God[1]; therefore the Creator, the God of the Old Testament, was not the true God. Now, with all his disagreement with Marcion, Tertullian is at one with him in this, that the Father is not referred to in these passages, but Christ the Son. Some Old Testament references could be expounded of the Father, who is "invisible and unapproachable and at rest, and so to speak, the God of the philosophers"; on the other hand, those to which the Marcionites took exception "will be reckoned as applying to the Son who was seen and heard, who walked with men, the witness and minister of the Father, mingling in Himself man and God, in His powers God, in His weaknesses man, so as to confer on man as much as He takes from God. In a word, all that you regard as uncomely in my God is the Sacrament of human salvation[2]."

A full discussion of the position adopted by Tertullian in refutation of Marcionites and Patripassians would belong to a detailed study of his theology. But at least it may be said that the distinction drawn in the *Adversus Praxeam*[3] between the divine and human *substantiae* in Christ, with the corollary that since the one is immortal and the other mortal He died "as flesh and Son of man, not as Spirit and Word and Son of God," does not give us the whole of his thought. Dorner is a true, if, perhaps, rather too rigorous an interpreter when he says

[1] *E.g.* the question to Adam, "Where art thou?" *Adv. Marc.* II, 25.
[2] *Ibid.* II, 27.   [3] c. 29.

"all the finitude, all the passibility, which the Patripassians attributed to God in general, or to the Father,
he transfers to the Son[1]." Tertullian's doctrine is
further advanced and his terminology far more adequate
than anything to be found among the Apologists; nor
does Irenaeus give the same impression of completeness
as that afforded by the monograph against Praxeas. But
the standpoint of the Apologists, relative to cosmology,
which drove them in the direction of ditheism, with the
Son as a subordinate hypostasis, is still his standpoint. The
generation of the Word as Son is associated with the
purpose of world-creation. In the treatise *Adversus
Hermogenem* he not only denies the eternity of the relationship Father-Son in God, but also definitely opposes
to the Gnostic's doctrine of an eternal matter, in readiness
for the creation of the world, the doctrine of the
generation of Wisdom in God "when God perceived
the necessity of wisdom for the construction of things
in the world[2]." The position thus assigned to the Word,
which is that of the principle intermediary between God
and creation, though substantially one with God, is one

---

[1] Div. i, vol. ii, p. 69. Adhemar D'Ales in his treatise,
La Théologie de Tertullian, pp. 75–103, does not allow that
what Tertullian says implies anything less transcendent in the
Son's Deity than in the Father's as regards relationship to the
world. It is true that Tertullian, in *Adv. Prax.* 14, asserts
that the Son, in respect of His divinity, is invisible. But D'Ales
admits that there is a subordinationistic element in some of
Tertullian's expressions, and these suggest that more was
intended than D'Ales concedes by the distinction in *Adv. Prax.*
15 between the eternal absolute invisibility of the Father and
the often-repeated visibility of the Son.

[2] *Adv. Herm.* 18.

which makes it possible for Tertullian to see a fitness and, indeed, a possibility, of certain experiences in connexion with the Son which would have been out of place if assigned to the Father. The main points in Tertullian's dogmatic scheme reappear in Novatian's work *On the Trinity*. There is the same explanation of the Old Testament theophanies with the proof, concisely given, but with a definiteness of logic that goes beyond the earlier theologian, that it is impossible that such appearances should have been of the Father, since He who encloses every place and contains all things cannot be thought of as moving from place to place[1]. There is the same assertion of the unity between the Father and the Son in respect of substance, coupled with the subordinationism that arises from the notion of the Son being generated at the Father's will, with a view to the creation of the world. There is the same comparison between the invisibility of the Father and the visibility of the Son. For Novatian a doctrine of the natural invisibility of the Son is equivalent to a doctrine of "two invisibles and so of two Gods[2]." At the same time, because the Godhead of the Son is true Godhead, and everyone understands "that Godhead is impassible, but human weakness is passible," language such as "God has died," which heretics of the Theodotian and Artemonite school used as descriptive of the logical, but absurd, position, reached by those who maintained that Christ was not man only but also God, does not fairly represent the orthodox belief. Not the divine, but the

[1] *De Trin.* 17.
[2] *Ibid.* 31.

human taken up into union with the divine died in Him[1].

But apart from positions expounded by Novatian in relation to Trinitarian and Christological dogma and to the controversies of the time, there is one chapter in which he discusses the question of the feelings which may be ascribed to God, somewhat after the fashion of the chapter[2] in the second book of the treatise against Marcion, but more fully. He has just described God as immortal and incorruptible, of a perfection which admits of no diminution. What then of the anger and hatred we read of as felt by Him? We must not look for an explanation in what we know of such things as human vices: "for all those things, though they can corrupt man, cannot at all impair the divine power; while they will be rightly spoken of as passions in man they will not be rightly regarded as passions in God. For through them man can be corrupted since he is capable of corruption, but God cannot be corrupted by them, since He is incorruptible. The power which they may exercise they possess therefore only where a passible material is precedent to them, not where an impassible substance is precedent."

---

[1] *De Trin.* 25. Terminology became of greater importance under the pressure of controversy and as it became necessary to distinguish sharply the doctrine of the Church from that of either wing of the Monarchians. One may observe that when Dorner remarks (Div. I, vol. II, pp. 69 f.) that Tertullian does not entirely deny the passibility of God he refers to the *De Carne Christi*, 5, for the use of such expressions as *passus mortuus est Deus*. But there Tertullian says not *Deus* but *Filius Dei*.

[2] *Adv. Marc.* II, 16.

God's anger, hatred, and feelings of that kind come from no fault in Him, but have a remedial purpose, to recall man to the good. Human nature is made up of a diversity of material; hence, in man, anger leads to discord and corruption. But God is wholly simple and spirit; there is nothing material, with its consequent corruptibility, in Him. His feelings proceed not from any flaw, but from reason[1].

What Novatian means is that in God there is a perfect concord between feeling and reason which is not to be found in man, especially not in the case of such feelings as anger and hatred. In the *passiones* of humanity there is something destructive. When we think how for us the word "passions" carries us to a further point than the word "feelings," we realize what Novatian is trying to express. We speak of "the passions being under control," implying that the emotional forces inherent in them cannot safely be allowed to give free expression to their nature. Close attendant upon, if not inherent in, the idea of the passionate is the idea of something irrational. And then we have only to recall the place which Reason occupied in ancient systems of philosophy[2], and the importance

[1] *De Trin.* 5.
[2] Plato, Aristotle and the Stoics exalted the principle of reason above everything else in their various accounts of human nature. As a parallel with what Novatian says about anger reference may be made to the *Republic*, VIII, 586 c, E, where Plato argues that no satisfaction is to be obtained in anger if it is pursued "apart from reason and mind." Weber (*History of Philosophy*, pp. 128 f., Eng. tr.), interpreting Aristotle's doctrine of man, points out the preeminence for Aristotle of

of the Logos-doctrine, when Christianity made its claim to be the one adequate philosophy of religion, to realize the way in which a theologian with any philosophical background would be likely to speak when treating of the emotions ascribed in any authoritative literature to God. Moreover, it was quite in accord with the position held by the conception of substance that the effect of emotion should be considered in relation thereto. The divine substance, as simple and eternal, was necessarily impervious to the disintegrating tendencies of the passions. A change in it would be a change from the good to the less good, an incredible supposition. We must always bear in mind in connexion with deductions made in the sphere of that primary theology which is the doctrine of God, that they represent not only positive truths but also bulwarks against paganism. To suppose that Christian thinkers carelessly passed over all that seems to us involved in our belief in God's loving care, His fatherly providence, and His moral purposefulness, would be the greatest injustice both to their words and to their thought.

At this point the chronological order may be deserted, and a consideration of the teaching of the Alexandrine theologians postponed, in order to link up with Tertullian and Novatian the later Western writers Arnobius

"the active intellect (νοῦς ποιητικός)." It is the one divine, immaterial and impassible thing in man. It alone is able to conceive the universal and the divine and "enjoy the privilege of immortality." For Stoicism the human ideal is the wise man, who is wholly rational. So in his *Hymn* Cleanthes speaks of the noble life as the intelligent obedience to the one rational principle (λόγος) of all things.

and Lactantius who prolong into the fourth century the tradition of Western apologetic.

The contrast between paganism and Christianity could, as we have seen, be stated with great effect in the opposed conceptions of the divine nature. Arnobius develops his argument in the approved way, though with an original idea of his own when he contemplates the possibility of the gods being real though inferior deities, the offspring of the one true God, "through whom, if they exist, they have begun to be, and to receive the substance of their divinity and majesty[1]," and of whose will it is that they either perish or are endowed with immortality, since by nature they are corruptible and destructible. That this is so is manifested by the hostility to Christianity which pagans attributed to their gods. If it is indeed true that the gods are afire with anger, then they cannot be regarded as immortal or in any way divine—he means with the characteristics proper to true divinity. "For where there is any state of desire there of necessity must be passion. Where passion has its seat, there it is agreed that emotional agitation must follow, and where there is emotional agitation there is grief and sickness. Where grief and sickness are found, there now appears a place for diminution and corruption, and to those two vexations dissolution is a near neighbour, even death which ends everything and takes away life from all sentient existences[2]." Elsewhere Arnobius addresses the true God in words which show how natural, in reaction from the monstrous and incredible anthropomorphisms of the old mythology,

[1] *Adversus nationes*, i, 28.　　[2] *Ibid.* i, 17–18.

was the *via negativa* for expressing the perfection of God. "Thou art," he says, "infinite, unbegotten, immortal, perpetual, the only One whom no bodily form describes, no finitude of qualities limits, transcending every quantitative notion, without place, without motion, without guise, of whom nothing can be said and expressed according to the meaning of human language; we must be silent in order that Thou mayest be understood; and that conjecture may in its wanderings be able to trace Thee through the shadows, nothing at all must be uttered[1]." When he comes to speak of the Crucifixion, this strong feeling of the impropriety of ascribing such an experience as death to one who is truly God, though with that measure of relative inferiority in His Godhead which belongs to Him in virtue of the fact that He is not Himself the "Supreme King," leads Arnobius to say "It was not He Himself who was cut off; for the occasion of death cannot come upon divine realities, nor, through the dissolution which attends upon perishing can that slip away which is one and simple and not compacted by any assemblage of parts. The one who died was the man whom He had put on, whom He bore along with Him[2]."

Lactantius is of greater interest because, while he asserts in a manner similar to that of his teacher Arnobius, the perfection of God, His incorruptibility, impassibility

[1] *Adv. nat.* I, 31; cf. III. We must not even ascribe such virtues as courage and wisdom and intelligent provision to God. These are human excellences.

[2] *Ibid.* I, 61. In this passage "homo" must be translated "man"; but the passage which precedes this one shows that Arnobius conceived of no personal dualism in Christ.

and freedom from all external control, and His transcendence alike of human conceptions and human language[1], he devotes a special treatise to the subject of the divine anger. His intention is to argue against those who think "that God is moved by no feeling[2]," and in particular deny that anger has any place in Him, though some would allow His graciousness. But the more logical procedure is, with Epicurus, to deny both, since, as that philosopher saw, the obverse of what he held to be the vice of anger was the virtue of graciousness or good pleasure. This is equivalent, says Lactantius, to denying God's existence, since movement is characteristic of everything that has life. Moreover, how can God be blessed, if He is in a state of torpor, ever at rest and without motion, deaf to prayers and blind to His worshippers? And if there is no feeling at all in God, the whole notion of His providence disappears[3]. The final result of the Epicurean position is, for Lactantius, the disappearance of religion, which cannot last if the idea either of God's graciousness or of His anger is abandoned[4], and this he regards as the outcome of the positions reached by the philosophers and poets who, while confessing one supreme God, "since they believe that He is always beneficent and free from the corruption of passions, think that He is neither angry with anyone nor needs any worship. So religion cannot exist where there is no fear[5]."

[1] *Epitome inst. divin.* 3.　　　[2] *De ira Dei,* 2.
[3] *Ibid.* 4.　　　　　　　　　　[4] *Ibid.* 8.
[5] *Ibid.* 11. *Incorruptum* carries the same implications as we have already noticed in connexion with Novatian. The argument

The more positive part of the treatise begins with
a discussion of Epicurus' argument that "if in God there
is a feeling of happiness issuing in graciousness, and of
hate issuing in anger, He must also be the subject of
fear, and lust and all the other feelings which belong to
human weakness." Lactantius, in his reply, distinguishes
the feelings according as they have or have not any
material[1] for their existence in God. Fear has none,
since He cannot be subjected to any compulsion or
experience any of those losses which provide the
material for the existence of fear in man. Nor is there
material for the existence of lust or envy or avarice
in God: "but graciousness and anger and pity have
material for their existence in God, and rightly does that
supreme and unique Power use them for the preservation of things made[2]. The material for pity is to be found
in human afflictions, for God's graciousness in human
prayers and offerings and good works, for anger in
wickedness and neglect of God[3]." He returns to another
point in Epicurus' doctrine, that God exercises no
providential care, but is free from corruption, and
blessed, because always at rest. Absolute rest, he replies,
is in death alone, so that it cannot be attributed to God.
And God's action must take the form of governing the
world, and so of care for the life of men. God wishes
men to act wisely and rightly, and since this is His will
and the divine law, His anger must be stirred against
those who set it at nought; it would be the reverse of

which Lactantius has to meet is that such emotions as anger have
a destructive effect upon substance.
[1] *Materia.*   [2] *De ira Dei*, 15.   [3] *Ibid.* 16.

goodness in Him, as human analogy shows, were it not so. The Stoics went wrong in not distinguishing between just and unjust anger. This latter, which needs checking in man, cannot exist in God at all, since God cannot suffer harm[1]. But just anger, directed to moral ends, has a place in God. For God ought to check the sins of all men, and that He should do this it is necessary for Him to be angry, since it is natural for one who is good to be moved and stirred in opposition to another's sin. So the definition which ought to have been given of anger is "anger is the movement of the mind as it rises up to check sins[2]." This anger is entirely in God's control, so that "He is not ruled by it, but Himself restrains it just as He pleases[3]," and abides as eternal only against those who sin eternally.

Lactantius' monograph is interesting as the first specific attempt, of which we have knowledge, to deal with a question which gives rise to perplexity in some quarters to-day, just as it had done centuries before the *De ira Dei* was written. The author argues his case, as a whole, reasonably and well. He is indeed far too much influenced by the belief that if the motive of fear is taken away men will cease to be religious[4], but the deeper justification of the ascription of anger to God lies in his conviction that anger represents an indispensable moral element in the divine nature, and that to rule out all

---

[1] Which, it is implied, results from unjust anger.
[2] *De ira Dei*, 17. [3] *Ibid.* 21.
[4] The last chapter gives an amazing example of this, which is almost the exact opposite of the truth contained in the words "Whose service is perfect freedom."

emotional reaction in God under the plea of maintaining unimpaired certain supposedly physical necessities of the divine life is to evacuate that life of reality.
A God who is literally and altogether *quietus* and
immobilis is not really anything at all. To deny the
sufficiency of such descriptions is not to subject God to
any external control, since the principle of motion
resides in His own nature and finds expression in the
necessary moral attitude in which God places Himself
towards good and evil respectively.

3. ALEXANDRINE THEOLOGY

We will now return to the School of Alexandria.
Its philosophical associations with idealism, its great
stress on the importance of the true γνῶσις and on the
Christian Gnostic as displaying the highest type of
personality, its corresponding indifference to, or rather
aversion from, the emotional elements in life as representing the irrational side of human nature, its readiness
on occasion to make use of the *via negativa* as a means
for expressing the absolute transcendence of God, and,
finally, its allegorical method in exegesis, all combine to
enlist its natural sympathies in a strong emphasis on the
side of the importance of the conceptions of the divine
unchangeableness and impassibility. It is interesting to
note that of the very minute fragments reproducing his
opinions which constitute all the material we have for
direct insight into the mind of Clement's master, the
first head of the catechetical school, Pantaenus, one is
relevant to the question of God's relationship to the
world. The master, we are told, and his circle, denied

that God knew according to the method of the intellect things that belonged to the intellect, or according to the method of the senses things that belonged to the senses; "for it is not possible that He who transcends existences should apprehend existences by means of (κατά) existences; but we say that He knows existences as the products of His own acts of will, adducing in support of this a reasonable argument; for if by His will He has created all things, to which there can be no objection, and it is always pious and right to say that God knows His own will, and with an act of will He has created each thing that has been brought into existence, then it follows that God knows existences as the products of His own acts of will, since with His will He has created these existences[1]." If all relationship of God to the world except one of transcendent causality is denied, as this passage seems to suggest, it is difficult to see how any place can be left for a reaction upon the divine life from the side of creation. It may be said that the knowledge of existences as the products of His will (ὡς ἴδια θελήματα) is simply knowledge of the fact of their existence, and that Pantaenus did not mean to imply that every condition of a thing's being or every relationship in which it might be found expressed the divine will. We do not know enough of the context to be certain, though it seems to have been concerned in some way with the question of predestination, but the passage as a whole is not favourable to the notion of any such contact with the finite as must be the background of any belief in the possibility of God.

[1] Routh, *Rel. Sac.* I, p. 379.

In Clement the connexion of the Christian with the philosopher or the student of philosophy is one in which it is not always easy for the former to maintain his rights. If the latter gains too much control, the belief in the Incarnation is robbed of its proper setting in a doctrine of God's providence and love. So it is in the passage in the *Stromateis* in which Clement asserts the impossibility of naming God, since no logical division, genus and so forth, is applicable in His case. And the religious names given to Him, Father or God or Lord are, in no case, His real name, but good substitutes for it[1]. Clement is not quite as generous in his estimate of Greek philosophy as might at first sight appear, for along with his recognition of the real value to be found in some of its schools there appears the notion that the truths which such philosophers as Pythagoras and Plato taught were taken from Moses[2]. But he was greatly influenced by it, and, so far as his metaphysical outlook is concerned, especially in connexion with the doctrine of God. "If," he says, "we exclude all that belongs to bodies, and all that belongs to what is called incorporeal, and should cast ourselves into the greatness of Christ, and thence should proceed from holiness to immensity, we should in some way attain to the conception of the Almighty, knowing not what He is but what He is not[3]."

[1] *Strom.* v, 12.
[2] Cf. *Ibid.* v, 5, where the light of Greek philosophy is compared to that of the wick kindled by men who have stolen the light from the sun, and 1, 22, where Clement quotes the famous rhetorical question of Numenius of Apamaea: "What is Plato but Moses speaking Greek?"
[3] *Ibid.* v, 11.

It is this kind of language which leads M. de Faye to say that Clement's God, metaphysically considered, is a mere negation, and that the influence of philosophy upon Clement was rationalistic[1]. That Clement, standing as he does, at the very beginning of the attempts to construct a Christian philosophy of religion, should not have been successful in combining ideas of God which rest upon a basis of abstractions and form themselves into a doctrine of the Absolute with a theology which claims to find in the religious and moral relationships in which God stands to men the surest clue to the understanding of the divine nature is not surprising. That still remains, and is likely to remain, a not completely soluble problem.

Clement several times asserts God's freedom from everything emotional. In the passage in the fifth book of the *Stromateis* to which reference has already been made, he argues that both where the divine anger and threatenings are spoken of and in allusions to God's bodily members there can be no intention to ascribe affections ($\pi \acute{a}\theta\eta$) to God. An allegorical meaning is to be sought[2]. For Clement, to be raised above passion is the ideal set before the Christian Gnostic, the deification which corresponds to that permanent condition of God who is "without passion, without anger, without desire," not, in His case, by conquest and control of emotions such as fear, anger and the like, but because His life is one and immutable in the possession of all good things[3]. The mixture of Christian elements with

---

[1] *Clément d'Alexandrie*, pp. 214–30, 297.   [2] *Strom.* v, 11.
[3] *Ibid.* iv, 23; cf. ii, 18. To be made like to the Lord is "to

such as spring from a noble and austere ethical philosophy that lacks the true humanity of Christianity, in Clement's conception of the ideal Christian man, the true Gnostic, is clearly given in the remarkable chapters in which he depicts the Gnostic's life[1]. Alongside of all the excellent instruction which he gives on the Christian's faithfulness and self-control, his purity, and, above all, on his love of God "the most holy and sovereign science of all," there runs the notion of passionlessness as in and for itself a supreme moral excellence. The advanced Christian will be out of the reach not only of the wrong sort of pleasurable emotions, but of all pleasurable emotions. "He is the truly good man, he who is outside the passions, having overcome the whole of the life of passion by some habit or condition of his soul endowed with virtue"; no pleasure will he look for through the senses, "since he is suspicious even of a word which brings pleasure, of a movement of thought, of an agreeable activity"; and, "he who is not willing to cut away the passion of the soul, kills himself." Everything that belongs to his life in this world Clement's Gnostic does, not because it is pleasant, but in so far as it is necessary, and his perfection will consist in "forgiving sins, forgetting injuries and living in the habit of passionlessness." This is a view of life certainly different from that in which man believes that God gives him all things richly to enjoy, and, despite become just and holy and understanding also. For the divine nature needs nothing and is without passions, wherefore it is not rightly called self-controlled. For no passion ever besets it for it to control. But our nature admits of passion and so needs control."   [1] *Strom.* VII, 11–14.

Clement's exposition of it, it represents an impoverished Christian ethic[1].

One particular chapter, the ninth of the sixth book of the *Stromateis*, deserves close attention, both because of its bearing on Clement's general conception of the emotions and of the relation of the Christian to them, and because with that is associated a closely related Christological doctrine. The Gnostic, he begins by saying, is subject only to those affections ($\pi\acute{a}\theta\eta$) which, like hunger, are necessary for the preservation of the body. In the case of the Saviour it would be absurd to conceive of any such necessity. He took food only in order to prevent those who were with Him falling into the Docetic error which came in at a later date. "He was altogether impassible, into Him no movement of passion could find its way, neither pleasure nor pain." The Apostles, through His teaching, not only triumphed over anger and fear and desire, but attained such a state of stability that, at least from the Lord's Resurrection onwards, they were subject to no emotional change, so that not even the emotions which seem good, courage, zeal, joy, desire could be attributed to them. Nothing can affect the perfect man so as to evoke any of these emotions. He lacks nothing and desires nothing, and for these reasons he is compelled to be made like to the Teacher in respect of impassibility, and the secret of this affinity is the divinity of love which the Gnostic

---

[1] For the idea of the passions as the enemy to be overcome, cf. *Strom.* vii, 3, "he is the true athlete, who in the great arena, the beautiful world, is crowned by reason of the true victory over all the passions."

possesses and in which he abides unchangeably. And since of no single passion can there be any need in the case of him "who has gained the kinship with the impassible God which springs from love, and through love has enrolled himself among His friends, our Gnostic and perfect man must be freed from every affection of the soul. For knowledge is the cause of practice, and practice of habit or disposition; and such a condition produces passionlessness, not moderation of passion; yea, passionlessness is the fruit of the perfect eradication of desire." So the whole of the emotional side of life is dead for the Gnostic. He may not speed his physical dissolution, "but he has withdrawn his soul from the passions, for this is permitted to him."

One point of special interest, and, indeed, difficulty, arrests the attention in Clement's delineation of the perfect Christian. Such a man is filled with love, and the place which love has, dominant and controlling, in his character, enables us to distinguish the Christian saint from the Stoic sage. But so far is this love from being in any sense an affection or emotion of the soul that Clement can make use of it to show how its presence secures the Christian against the passions. Whereas the passions involve inner movement and instability, love is the fixed state of the Gnostic life. It is obvious that Clement would feel no need to reconcile his notion of the divine impassibility with his belief that Christ suffered because of His love towards us[1]. And so we are left with the curious conclusion that while in Christ a place must be left for the reality of His bodily suffering,

[1] *Strom.* vi, 8.

since Clement could not deny that without going over consciously and deliberately into the Docetic camp, no kind of emotional impulse is to be regarded as affecting in any way His soul. We must think of the Lord as being "without beginning, impassible," as "assuming flesh which is by nature passible and training it to a condition of impassibility[1]." The religious value of Christ's sufferings is hard to preserve when the emotions are regarded as essentially hostile to the soul's apprehension of the good.

Both in the *De Principiis* and in the *Contra Celsum* Origen speaks of the emotions, so far as their attribution to God is concerned, in a way which is in line with the teaching of Clement. In the former work he has been arguing against dualists of the type of Marcion that the God of the Old Testament is one and the same God as the Father of Christ. He proceeds[2] to deal with the objection that whereas God is "wholly impassible," and cannot be regarded as the subject of any such human affection as anger or repentance (a position which is clearly common ground in the dispute), these feelings are attributed to the Deity of the Old Testament. His answer, for which in a more expanded form he refers to his commentary on Psalm ii, 5[3], is that such expressions are not to be taken literally but that we must look for

---

[1] *Strom.* VII, 2.   [2] *De Prin.* II, 4. 4.

[3] Origen's commentary on this verse as we have it in the *Selections on the Psalms* which have been preserved does not deal precisely with the meaning of anger and wrath. But there is a suggestion of the "spiritual meaning" in the interpretation of these feelings as intended to bring the objects of them to repentance.

the spiritual meaning involved. In his great apologetic work Origen deals with the matter more fully. Celsus, who had ridiculed the scriptural language, had failed, so the reply begins, to understand that the sayings about God in the Scriptures were "as though God were subject to human affections." The wrath of God is an expression which ought not to be taken as implying the presence of any passion in God, "but we say that it is something assumed with a view to the discipline through sterner measures of those who had sinned often and grievously." Origen fortifies his opinion by appealing to the meaning and implications of various scriptural passages, and claims that the true figurative interpretation of such passages shows that "we do not therefore ascribe human passions to God, nor do we hold impious opinions about Him[1]." So far Origen might be regarded as simply of the same mind as Clement, but that is not the whole truth. Two passages referred to by Dr Bigg[2] give us another and a richer doctrine. One is found in the course of the homily on the sixteenth chapter of Ezekiel. Origen is illustrating the meaning of compassion from the motive of the Incarnation. "He descended to earth in pity for the human race, He suffered our sufferings, before He suffered the Cross and thought it right to take upon Him our flesh. For if He had not suffered, He would not have come to take part in human life. First did He suffer, then He descended and was seen. What is that passion which He suffered for us? Love is passion. The Father also

[1] *C. Cels.* IV, 71–2.
[2] In his *Christian Platonists of Alexandria,* p. 158.

Himself, and the God of all things, longsuffering and very pitiful and compassionate, does not He in some way suffer? Can you be ignorant of this, that when He deals with human things He suffers a human passion? 'For the Lord thy God endured thy ways as if a man should endure his son.' Therefore God endures our ways inasmuch as the Son of God bears our sufferings. The Father Himself is not impassible. If He is besought, He is pitiful and compassionate, He suffers something of love, and in those things in which because of the greatness of His nature He cannot subsist He shares[1], and because of us He endures human sufferings[2]." The other passage occurs in the homilies on the book of Numbers. There, commenting on the opening verses of the twenty-eighth chapter, Origen argues that God has His feast days when He rejoices over the salvation of those who believe and are converted: "wonderful perhaps it is what I wish to say; we give to God and the angels reasons for festivity and joy; we who are on earth give heaven its occasion for joy and exultation.... But as our good actions and our progress in virtue give birth to joy and festivity for God and the angels, so I fear lest our evil conversation be the cause of lamentations and sorrows not on earth only but in heaven as well, and lest the sins of men stir up sorrow perchance even for God Himself." Origen appeals to texts of Scripture in support of this suggestion, and further adds, "it is certain that where joy is felt for that which is good, there for that which is contrary thereto lamentation

---

[1] "Et fit in eis in quibus iuxta magnitudinem naturae suae non potest esse." [2] *In Ezech. Hom.* VI, 6.

follows: if therefore they rejoice over him who is converted, of necessity they must grieve for the sinner." But this passage, unlike the other one, closes with words which are intended to harmonize the position to which the development of his thought has led him with the doctrine of the divine ἀπάθεια: "now all these sayings in which God is spoken of as sorrowing or rejoicing or hating or being glad are to be understood as uttered by the Scripture after an allegorical and human manner. The divine nature is altogether separated from every affection of passion and change, and remains unmoved and unshaken forever on that peak of blessedness[1]." This conclusion, taken with all that precedes, is of great use in helping us to understand both the difficulties which beset the writers and theologians of the ancient Church when they were concerned with the emotions ascribed to God in the Bible, and also the special interest which they took in maintaining His passionlessness. It was certain that God was complete in His own nature and that nothing from without, from the created world, could affect that nature by adding to its perfection or taking anything from it. And to assert the reality of "passion" in God in such a way as not to expose His nature to a process of change which must imply a measure of deterioration was beyond their power. That the idea of "passion," while involving emotional movement within the divine nature, such movement as from joy to sorrow or *vice versa* in connexion with the moral and religious well-being of a section of the creation, whose being itself depends wholly

[1] *In Num. Hom.* XXIII, 2.

upon the divine will, need not mean a movement and change of the divine nature itself from the perfect to the less than perfect, was beyond their power to apprehend. Origen sees that such movements must be allowed for. And, after all, however "allegorical" the statement, it must be an allegory representing something real. But he gives up the attempt to hold together, or to show how a place may be found for, both the enduring blessedness of God in the perfection of His nature and a moral interest of God in the world, which can be represented as real only by attaching to it that flow of the emotions which is both the symbol and the expression of the varying moral judgments. That feeling in God is just the same as in man we must not say; our representations of the reality and the reality itself must be distinguished, though both the character and the measure of the distinction are outside any precision of description. But Origen's retreat within the fortifications of the allegorical method of Scripture cannot be ours.

The most important work which comes to us from the Alexandrine School after the writings of Clement and Origen himself is a dogmatic treatise of Gregory Thaumaturgus dealing explicitly with the question of the divine capacity for suffering, and of it a somewhat full account must now be given.

The treatise, which exists in Syriac and in Latin[1], begins with an account of the short preliminary question and answer which was to lead on to a lengthy treatment of the whole subject, the form of a dialogue being main-

[1] It is printed in Cardinal Pitra's *Sacra Analecta*, IV, pp. 103–20, 363–76.

tained throughout, but with less and less part being taken by the original questioner. Theopompus asks Gregory whether God is impassible, and Gregory replies "How can we say that God becomes subject to passion?" With his difficulties unresolved by this brief counter-question Theopompus follows Gregory and asks him to deal with the problem in more argumentative fashion. After a period of silence Gregory expresses his satisfaction at the renewal of the inquiry, and invites Theopompus to give his opinion on Gregory's answer. Theopompus then puts the dilemma as it appears to him, "if by nature God is impassible, it follows that He can never suffer, even though He should will (to suffer), since His nature would then be doing what was contrary to His will." Gregory protests against any subjection of God to necessity "by opposing His nature to His will. For if God does not do what He wills, it certainly follows that very great suffering befalls Him, since we should have to say that the will of God was subjected to His nature...we must understand that God is never prevented by His almighty nature from doing what He wills, since it befits us to say that God is superior to everything, and to nothing is He in subjection...it is impious to take away freedom from almighty God."

Theopompus in reply asserts that he is not trying to deny the divine freedom, but still is not satisfied. He restates the problem, "I ask whether God is not prevented by Himself from undergoing suffering, since He always is that which He is, if we consider the impassibility of His nature. I could wish...to learn... whether the impassible God can suffer anything incongruous with His nature, seeing that He is impassible as we have said. And further, I have been struck by the quite reasonable remark of certain persons that, since the nature of God is a barrier to His will, the question is futile. For if the impassibility of God does not suffer human sufferings, how should I not be able to answer you boldly, saying that the nature of God is in opposition to His will? Whence it follows, as I said before, that the nature of the impassible God is more powerful than His will, even though this is God."

Gregory now seeks a way out of the difficulty by drawing a distinction between man and his Creator. In man, owing to his constitution, there can be a clash between will and nature; "the human will cannot freely carry out whatever it contrives, since now the nature now the will draws man each to its own side." But God is free from every sort of constraint and defect, and so can do all things. We ought never to conceive of God "as though He were contrary to His own will, because He has subjected Himself to suffering, being by nature impassible. For we do not separate the will of the God-head from that most blessed essence, which always is as it is, remaining one and the same, in one form, in one being, in one unchangeable will; which learns of itself, gives orders to itself, and itself, of itself and in itself and through itself, is able to do all things, without the will being at any point prevented by the impassible nature from effecting what it wills, since at every time it is as it is." Further contrast between man and God follows; God is simple not composite, the unity of His essence involves freedom from any admixture of evil,

His will is one, good, indivisible, never overcome: "do not think," thus he ends this statement, "that He who possesses all things, is by no one subjected to sufferings and by no one withstood, is prevented from accomplishing what He will."

Once again Theopompus objects that in his answer, true though it is so far as it goes, Gregory has not gone to the heart of the difficulty. What he wants to know is, "whether the nature of the Godhead is not prevented by itself from suffering, and whether a substance which is impassible does not preclude its own will from undergoing suffering, since that would be quite alien to it and not benefit it." Could God ever have chosen to undergo human sufferings, seeing that impassibility is a constant fact of His nature?

Gregory now comes to the centre of his reply through an exposition of what is involved in *passio*. "Suffering then is truly suffering when God plans anything useless and of no advantage to Himself. But when the divine will is aroused with a view to the healing of the wicked thoughts of men, then we do not think of suffering as involved for God in the fact that of His supreme humility and kindness He becomes the servant of men.... In God those are not to be accounted as sufferings which of His own will were borne by Him for the common good of the human race, with no resistance from His most blessed and impassible nature. For in His suffering He shows His impassibility. For he who suffers suffers, when the violence of suffering brings pressure to bear on him who suffers contrary to his will. But of him who, while his nature remains impassible, is of his own will

immersed in sufferings that he may overcome them, we
do not say that he becomes subject to suffering, even
though, of his own will, he has shared in sufferings."
Just as a physician loses nothing of his dignity through
the assistance which he gives to the sick but gains
greater glory through his restoration to them of their
lost health, so what objection is there to saying of Him
who alone is good that "in His impassibility He extended His sceptre over the sufferings, since by His
suffering He has caused them to suffer? For He who
cannot suffer became the (cause of) suffering to the
sufferings, by bringing suffering upon them through
His suffering, and showing His freedom from suffering
in His suffering.... When therefore we say that sufferings were overcome through His working, from the
fact that He the Impassible became a sharer in them,
what else are we saying than that He was the cause of
suffering to sufferings?" Gregory illustrates his meaning by an analogy. When iron strikes adamant, the
adamant receives no hurt, but the blow recoils upon the
iron, "so shall we not say that God who is strong in
His will and impassible in His essence, when He has
accepted sufferings, has yet remained in His impassibility, even though tried by iron and fire, since the
nature of the Godhead is stronger than anything, even
when it is involved in sufferings?"

The relation of God to suffering is thus described as
a relation not of subjection but of triumph. Just as God
is "the death of death," so is He "the suffering of
sufferings." Suffering in God "does not occasion any
reproach or show any weakness, since the nature of God

more excellently displays its changelessness when it is tried by sufferings." Similarly "the coming of God to death clearly showed His divine power and impassibility of essence, since by death He was not held down...to God alone must we grant power over death. So God enters the gates of death and does nor suffer death." Another analogy, that of the flame-resisting Salamander, is given to show that there is nothing impossible in the thought of God sharing death, and, at the same time, displaying His impassibility. "How," asks Gregory with the idea of the necessary changelessness of the divine nature in his mind, "how would that most blessed Being not remain always the same, since His essence could suffer no hurt and His will no opposition or constraint? ...It is right to speak of sufferings in connexion with those things which are overcome by sufferings and are changed by corruption. But those things which come to pass through the excellent wisdom of God and the wonderful dispensation of divine providence are not to be regarded as sufferings of God, since nothing productive of suffering is discovered in them, by virtue of the impassibility of God's nature." Once more comes an earthly analogy; the substance of fire remains the same and suffers no separation when cut by a sword, "though body passes through body," even so no hurt is done to the divine nature and its characteristics by whatever wishes to attack it.

Thus, with the divine impassibility a constant fact, even when God of His own will takes upon Him human sufferings, since that does not involve for God "the sorrows which come from human sufferings," the divine changelessness is equally preserved. But change-lessness does not mean inactivity and aloofness. A God who "despised all other things because of the excellence of the rest which He had chosen for Himself" would be inferior to the famous self-sacrificing heroes of Greece. But in point of fact "God who does not need glory, who is superior to sufferings, He, of His own choice, came to death without fear or terror assailing Him." There was nothing shameful in a death whose object was to free men from death. God "showed His power over all things, by breaking death's tyranny, and spoiling death of that lordship wherewith it rejoiced over all things. But the nature of God in death remained un-corrupt, and by virtue of His impassibility He put to flight the sufferings, even as the light which mingles with the darkness." The substance of the incorruptible God remains impassible even when it is brought into close relations with things that bring suffering with them.

Gregory appeals to Theopompus not to believe that the most blessed Being is one who does nothing and gives no power of action to another. If God were careless of man and had no desire to do good, then indeed should we have to ascribe *passio* to Him, and that in the highest degree. "But He who pursues the corruptions of suffering (*passionum*) to their very root, that is, in the human mind, and by His providential dispensations makes men endowed with virtue good after they have been bad, how shall He not be called impassible, seeing that He drives away *passio* from men, and brings death upon it?" In the next section Gregory continues his appeal, insisting that, "He is most blessed and the giver of good things who is the helper of men and the strengthener of those who have no hope." In helping man God has become subject to no suffering or weakness. God would not allow men to perish without coming to their help. The philosophers point to the true way. It was their object in life to attend especially to those who were immersed in suffering. And if it has been true of the philosophers, how much more of God "Who is the teacher of all philosophy"?

And so Gregory comes to his last words, "Jesus, who is King over all, came to heal the difficult diseases of mankind, as a Being most blessed, and generous in His good deeds[1]. He, remaining what He was, made void sufferings by His impassibility, even as the light drives away darkness. He came, then, He came hastening to make men blessed and filled with good things, to make out of mortals immortals, to renew and establish them at last in their blessedness. To Him be glory, who is the King glorious for ever! Amen."

This third century treatise, rightly regarded, according to very competent authorities, as the work of Gregory Thaumaturgus, raises a number of quite fundamental questions in connexion with the problem to which it is devoted. Thus, it is clear that no theistic philosopher can be content with any idea of a real opposition between nature and will in God. Yet, supposing that God wills to suffer, how, in view of the fact that such suffering must take place within the divine nature, can any conclusion be avoided which would subject the divine nature to suffering through

[1] Or "lavish of the goods which He possesses."

some particular reactions of external circumstance upon God? How can we affirm that suffering is wholly within the divine control? But any development of such questions or of the ideas which derive from them will lead on to an analysis of "suffering," so that it may enable us to realize what we do and do not assert in affirming or denying the passibility of God. Gregory certainly regards anything of the nature of unpleasantly-toned emotion as no part of the *passio* which God takes upon Himself. Nevertheless, that is not the point on which he lays the greatest stress. What he is particularly concerned to say is that *passio* may be predicated of God when the experiences which God takes upon Himself are directed by God's will to a good end, and display not any weakness on the part of God, but His power and triumph. Gregory may not have found the exact point at which it is necessary to limit any ascription of *passio* to God; nevertheless, he has opened out and set foot upon an important line of advance to a true understanding of the problem. Further, Gregory makes what is, in effect, the valuable suggestion that we must not sacrifice the idea of God's moral action and of the love from which His energy proceeds to a supposed necessity for maintaining a metaphysical conception of the quiescence of the divine life. Gregory's stress is on the *Semper Agens* rather than on the *Semper Quietus*, or, perhaps, it would be more truly said that he thinks of God as at rest, without prejudice to and in the midst of the divine activity. In his emphasis upon the worthiness of God's self-donation for the salvation of men Gregory carries forward the apologetic of which Origen had made use in his reply to Celsus, an apologetic which goes back to the New Testament and to the foundations underlying the construction of Christian theology. What Gregory has said in this connexion will remain a "true word" for those who wish to show that belief in the Incarnation and the Passion of the Son of God is one which does no injustice to the religious conviction of the blessedness and perfection of God.

Before we pass from the third century, a few other statements of the theologians of this period may be noticed. Dionysius of Alexandria, in a fragment preserved by Eusebius, one of a number which have come down to us from the defence which he made of his orthodoxy in respect of the Godhead of the Son, argues against certain theories of a Gnostic or Manichaean kind which ascribed to matter this measure of likeness to God, of being like Him, unoriginate, while allowing that its direction and ordering was at God's disposal. Dionysius replies that such a combination of likeness and unlikeness to God is incredible. "Let them," he continues, "give the reason why, if both are unoriginate, God is impassible, immutable, immoveable, active in work, but matter on the contrary subject to passion, changeable, unstable, experiencing modification[1]." In the qualities which it could not be denied that matter possessed, Dionysius saw the clear proof of its essential dissimilarity to God. In another Alexandrine theologian, Theognostus, we can see a preparatory approach towards the dogmatic affirmation of the unchangeableness of the

[1] Text in *The Letters and other Remains of Dionysius of Alexandria*, ed. C. L. Feltoe, p. 184.

Son which finds a place in the Nicene anathema. In a fragment from the *Hypotyposes* he asserts that the Logos "one Himself, and retaining in its integrity His likeness to the One, will thus be unchangeable, being the copy of the unchangeable Father. That which completely inclined to likeness to the One can never experience a change[1]."

The contrast between God and matter, which the extract from Dionysius sets forth, appears again in Methodius, and also with a controversial reference in his work *On Created Things*, in which he argued, against Origen's thesis of an eternal world, that "the passionless God is not changed through the creation of the world[2]." And in fragments of his work which have been preserved we have the kind of statement as to the suffering of the Incarnate Christ which we meet with later in the *Dogmatic Letter* of Cyril of Alexandria. For Methodius, the union in Christ of the invulnerable and impassible Wisdom with a humanity capable of suffering can be expressed only in paradox: "with power He suffered remaining impassible," "in the passible He remained impassible[3]."

[1] See L. B. Radford's *Three Teachers of Alexandria*, p. 26. The fragment was circulated by Diekamp in 1902.

[2] *On Created Things*, 3.

[3] These expressions are found in fragments of a homily, *De Cruce et Passione Christi*, Migne, *P.G.* XVIII, pp. 398–403.

4. ARIANISM AND THE CHRISTOLOGICAL
CONTROVERSIES

The Arian Controversy did not involve any clash of
opinions as to the divine nature, in so far as both sides
affirmed it to be free from all change and passion.
Nevertheless, the sharp difference as to the nature of the
Son led to a good deal of stress being laid on the attribute
of ἀπάθεια, and the way in which the subject is treated
in passages of Athanasius is not without interest. The
Arian Christology, with its equating of the ideas of
creation and generation as essentially one in relation to
the activity of God, denied the Origenistic doctrine of the
eternal generation, and did so, partly at least, in the
interests of the passionlessness of God which that
doctrine was supposed to undermine. In what we have
left of Arius' own sentiments there is evidence of this.
Thus, in the letter to Alexander of Alexandria, quoted
at length by Athanasius, Arius and his friends affirm
that if such scriptural phrases as "I came forth from the
Father and am come" "be understood by some to mean
as if a part of Him, one in essence, or as an issue, then
the Father is according to them compounded and
divisible and alterable and material, and, as far as their
belief goes, He has the circumstances of a body, Who is
the Incorporeal God[1]." That the Homoousian doctrine
left room for Sabellian and Manichaean doctrines which
offended against the simplicity of the divine nature was,

[1] *De Syn.* 16. (Newman's tr. revised by Robertson in his
edition of select works of Athanasius in the *Nicene and Post-
Nicene Fathers*).

if not the definite contention, at least the suspicion of the Arians, and of that mass of Eastern bishops, so difficult to describe by any one satisfactory term, of whom Eusebius the historian was a typical, though exceptionally learned, member. Specially impious was it in Arius' opinion to speak of the Son as an "eructation" (ἐρυγήν), or a production (προβολήν)[1]. His "fellow-Lucianist," Eusebius of Nicomedia, in a letter to Paulinus of Tyre expresses very clearly the dread of any materialistic conception of the nature of God which was felt by the opponents of the doctrine taught by Alexander of Alexandria. "We have never heard," he writes, "that there are two unbegotten beings, nor that one has been divided into two, nor have we learned or believed that it has ever undergone any change of a corporeal nature; but we affirm that the unbegotten is one, and one also that which exists in truth by Him, yet was not made out of His substance, and does not at all participate in the nature or substance of the unbegotten, entirely distinct both in nature and in power, and made after perfect likeness both of character and power to the maker[2]." Eusebius of Caesarea, in his letter to his Church, explaining his ability to accept the Creed adopted by the Council, shows in like manner what great importance attached to the freeing of the word ὁμοούσιος from every kind of corporeal interpretation. The Emperor, according to Eusebius, explained that the Son "was not

[1] In his letter to Eusebius of Nicomedia *ap.* Theodoret, *Hist. Eccl.* 1, 5.
[2] *Ibid.* 1, 6, translation in the third volume of the *Nicene and Post-Nicene Fathers.*

called consubstantial in respect of any bodily affections
(πάθη), nor did He subsist from the Father by any
division or abscission. For the immaterial and intellectual and incorporeal did not admit of any bodily
affection, but it was fitting to conceive of such things in
a divine and ineffable way[1]."

There can be no doubt that many who were not
prepared to follow Arius in his assertion of the creature-
hood of the Logos, and to find no difference between
saying of the Son that He was begotten and saying that
He was created, were greatly troubled by the word
ὁμοούσιος. Whatever exactly happened at Antioch
in 269 when Paul of Samosata was condemned, the word
was disallowed by the Council, and possibly because
some sort of materialistic meaning was suffered to adhere
to it. So Athanasius reports the matter in the *De
Synodis*[2], and this objection which Arius and his
associates take to the word in their letter to Alexander
shows that such a view of the word's meaning was
possible. They condemn together the Valentinian doctrine of the Son as an "issue" (προβολή), the Manichaean dividing of the divine substance, so that the Son
is a "portion of the Father, consubstantial," Sabellius'
term "Son-Father" (υἱοπάτωρ), which also involves
a division of the Monad, and the metaphors used by
Hieracas to state the relationship of the Son to the
Father, "one torch from another, or as a lamp divided

---

[1] The letter is given in Theodoret, I, 12, and in Socrates,
Hist. Eccl. I, 8, and was appended by Athanasius to his work
De Decretis Nicaenis.
[2] c. 45.

into two[1]." Alexander of Alexandria in writing to his
namesake of Constantinople[2] thought it well to disown
in the most explicit fashion all such ideas which might
arise from, or, rather, be foisted on to, the belief in
Christ as the only-begotten Son of God. He is "not
after the manner of bodies, by severance or by emanation,
as Sabellius and Valentinus think, but ineffably and
inexpressibly."

Every kind of mutability and passion was denied by the
Arians in the case of the supreme God. As regards the
created Logos or Son there was no reason in principle to
rule out the possibility of change or passion. So, in the
Thalia, Arius said of the Son, "in nature, as all are, so also
is the Word Himself changeable, but by His own free will
He remains good, while He chooses; but when He chooses
He can Himself change, just as we can, since He is
changeable by nature[3]." On the other hand, on the
moral as well as on the metaphysical side it was natural
to emphasize some kind of distinction between the Son
as the "perfect creature" and all other creatures: the
readiness of Athanasius of Anazarbus to speak of Christ
as one of the hundred sheep[4] was too irreligious to meet
with general approval on the Arian side. Accordingly
we have the word ἄτρεπτος used by Arius and his
friends in relation to the Son, but the unchangeableness
is not something which belongs to the Son's οὐσία as
such, but is the result of the will of God, who "made

---

[1] *De Syn.* 16.   [2] In Theodoret, 1, 3.
[3] Quoted by Athanasius in *Or. C. Ar.* 1, 5 (ed. W. Bright).
[4] Referred to in the *De Synodis*, 17, of his great namesake,
who refers to his "extreme audacity."

Him subsist at His own will, unalterable and unchangeable[1]." But, as in Himself the Word possesses no
security against change, and is liable to experience what
the created world as a whole experiences, Tixeront[2]
legitimately argues that the Arian Christology would
not need to find a place for any soul in Christ other than
the Logos Himself "passible and changing," so that on
the Logos could be imposed "the emotions and the
weaknesses attributed by Scripture to the humanity of
Jesus."

The Arian position on all these points may be studied
in the arguments of the most notable literary representative of the school in the latter part of the fourth
century—Eunomius. In him the implications of
Arianism worked themselves out into that extreme but
logical conclusion which is known as Anomoeanism.
Gregory of Nyssa in Books IV–VI of his work against
Eunomius is largely concerned with the arguments
which, as used by Eunomius, were intended to safeguard
the passionlessness of God and to show that the Son was
not of one substance with the Father. The Anomoean
contended that community of nature between the
Father and the Son was excluded by its consequences in
a doctrine of generation that must involve passion; in
support of this he referred to the analogy of bodily
generation: "who is so...inattentive to the nature of
things," he asked, "as not to know that...the things
begotten are generated by passion, and those which beget

---

[1] *De Synodis*, 16, from the letter of Arius and others to
Alexander.
[2] *Histoire des Dogmes*, II, p. 27.

naturally have an action which is not pure, by reason of their nature being linked with passions of all kinds[1]?" As he refused to acknowledge an essential difference between the Son and the created world—"they say," according to Gregory, "He is of the same kind with the world"—he could no more predicate immutability of essence of the Son than of the world. Because the devil was by nature changeable, "the mutability of essence, moved either way at will, involves a capacity of nature that follows the impulse of determination, so as to become that to which its determination leads it. Accordingly they will define the Lord as being capable even of contrary dispositions, drawing Him down as it were to a rank equal with the angels, by the conception of creation[2]." As a creature the Son could, so Eunomius argued, be brought into existence without any passion on God's part, but to keep the idea of generation free from the idea of passion was impossible[3].

The issue at this point between Eunomius and Gregory concerns the possibility of admitting in the case of Christ a Sonship which carries with it no suggestion of a created being, while at the same time preserving the impassibility of the nature of God who is the Father of Christ. Eunomius denied the possibility and could admit in the case of the Son no distinction between the ideas of "generation," "making" and "creation"; each appellation is in place when applied to the essence of the Son; the Father is "Generator," "Maker" and

[1] Greg. Nyss. *adv. Eunom.* IV, I (Eng. tr. in *Nicene and Post-Nicene Fathers*, vol, v, Gregory of Nyssa).
[2] *Ibid.* IV, 2.   [3] *Ibid.* IV, 4.

"Creator[1]." Gregory had to show both that real distinctions were involved in the first of these terms as compared with the other two, and that no πάθος was introduced into the divine nature when the generation of the Son was regarded as excluding the notion of the creation of the Son. And it was necessary for him not only to show that the Father remained untouched by passion, but also that the Incarnation did not imply any subjection to passion of that divine nature which was in the Son. As to the former point, Gregory, following the language of the fourth Gospel[2], distinguishes between material and spiritual generation and argues that in the case of men this latter generation is free from passion, wherefore, *a fortiori*, an immaterial and passionless generation may be conceived of in the case of God. Moreover, if human passion in "that generation which is through the flesh" is to be taken as a standard for ascribing passion to God in the generation of the Son, the fact that passion attaches to men's acts of creation may equally be pressed to show that God cannot create without being subject to passion. But if (as Eunomius and the Arians did not doubt) God "creates without labour or matter, He surely also begets without labour or flux[3]."

With the argument that the facts of the Incarnation, in particular the Lord's sufferings, pointed to a diversity

---

[1] *Adv. Eunom.* iv, 6.   [2] St John i, 13; iii, 3.

[3] *Adv. Eunom.* iv, 4. On the differences between human and divine generation, the one involving ideas of matter and time, the latter needing "to be cleared of all such ideas," cf. i, 39.

of the essences of the Father and the Son Gregory deals in a later book. Here Gregory attaches a meaning to the word "passion," which, though not appertaining by right to the Greek word πάθος, helps, perhaps more than he realized, towards clear thinking on the problem of the divine impassibility, even outside of the dispensation of the Incarnation, in connexion with which he uses it. "Nothing," he says, "is truly 'passion' which does not tend to sin.... We give the name of passion only to that which is opposed to the virtuous unimpassioned state.... Of that, at least, which is truly passion, which is a diseased condition of the will, He was not a partaker.... But the peculiar attributes of our nature, which, by a kind of customary abuse of terms, are called by the name of 'passion,' of these we confess the Lord did partake, of birth, nourishment, growth, of sleep and toil, and all those natural dispositions which the soul is wont to experience with regard to bodily inconveniences, the desire of that which is lacking, when the longing passes from the body to the soul, the sense of pain, the dread of death, and all the like, save only such as, if followed, lead to sin." With this definition of "passion" we can understand how Gregory can say of the Incarnate Christ that He is not "because He is the Healer of our infirmities, to be deemed on this account to have been Himself passible." The work of Christ, "the dispensation of the Passion," He entered on "not by weakness of nature but by the power of His will." At the same time Gregory, with the aid of the now developed doctrine of the Two Natures in Christ, was able to rebut any argument which asserted that the sufferings of Christ involved

M 6

"dissimilarity of essence" between the Son and the Father "by the opposition of the passible to the impassible"; the absolute impassibility of the divine nature is not prejudiced by the fact that the Son submits to suffering and death, since "we say that, as God, the Son is certainly impassible and incapable of corruption: and whatever suffering is asserted concerning Him in the Gospel, He assuredly wrought by means of His human nature which admitted of such suffering[1]." So in one of his letters[2] he speaks of "that heavenly passionlessness which is peculiar to the Deity being...preserved both in the beginning and in the end of His life as Man."

The Christological controversies necessarily led to questions arising as to the character of the Lord's sufferings. That Christ really suffered was a belief impossible to surrender without the plainest disloyalty both to the New Testament and to all that the Church had stood for in its opposition to notions of a phantasmal, Docetic, humanity. At the same time the Godhead could not be conceived of as in any way passible. The thirteenth anathema of the First Council of Sirmium in 351 is directed against anyone who "hearing that the only begotten Son of God has been crucified should declare that His deity has undergone corruption or suffering or change or diminution or destruction[3]." Where the emphasis upon the reality of the human nature prevailed there was no difficulty in construing the method of the

---

[1] *Adv. Eunom.* VI, I.   [2] *Ep.* XVII.

[3] Hahn, *Symbole*[3], p. 198. I owe the reference to Dr Raven in his *Apollinarianism*, p. 98, and to his work I owe the knowledge of relevant passages in Hilary.

sufferings which Christ had undergone. But some examples of the thought and language of theologians who dealt with the subject between the Councils of Nicaea and Chalcedon will show the character of the interconnexion between Christology and belief in the divine impassibility and, perhaps, be illuminating as to the need for careful statement in respect of the latter idea.

We may start with the denial, in the anathema appended to the Creed of Nicaea, that the Son of God is τρεπτὸς ἢ ἀλλοιωτός. This is involved in the belief that He is ὁμοούσιος τῷ πατρί. What is true of the Father Who is God must be true of the Son Who is not less truly God. If unchangeableness is a characteristic of the divine essence that will apply to the Son Who is of the essence of the Father, and one with Him in essence. Alexander of Alexandria, writing to his namesake of Constantinople, had drawn attention to the Arian position at this point, and opposed to it the conviction that the Son "is by nature immutable, perfect and all-sufficient[1]." Of Christological doctrine, in the strict sense, there is little in this letter, but Alexander refers to the reality of the body which our Lord took ἐκ τῆς θεοτόκου Μαρίας and to His crucifixion and death, while "yet for all this He suffered no diminution of His Godhead."

From the treatise *De Incarnatione* onwards, Athanasius had occasion from time to time in his works to show that the sufferings of Christ were in no way incompatible with the fullness of deity being His. In that early treatise he speaks of the Logos, "since it was im-

---

[1] Theodoret, *Hist. Eccl.* I, 3.

possible for Him to die, inasmuch as He is immortal and
the Son of the Father," taking to Himself a body which
could die "and, because of the Word which was come
to dwell in it, remain incorruptible[1]" (ἄφθαρτον), an
apparent paradox whereby Athanasius seeks to do justice to the fact that the body was a true body, and also
the body of the Logos. In the anti-Arian Orations the
questions appear to which, as we have seen in connexion
with the arguments of Eunomius, the Arian positions
necessarily drew attention, concerning the relation of
the generation of the Son to the divine passionlessness
and concerning the meaning of the experiences of the
Incarnate Christ. Of the absence of all passion from
God he speaks very clearly in passages of the Orations.
Thus, in the first Oration, God is said to be "not composed of parts, but being impassible and simple He is
impassibly and indivisibly Father of the Son[2]." Are the
Arians not mad, he asks, "in seeking and conjecturing
parts and passions in the instance of the immaterial and
true God, and ascribing divisions to Him who is beyond
passion and change[3]?" Even in the natural world, he
affirms, the idea that offspring implies partition of the
original essence does not always hold good. It was necessary for Athanasius to emphasize this part of his argument, since, as an Arian letter to Alexander makes clear,
the Arians interpreted the Homoousian doctrine as
equivalent to a Manichaean materialism[4]. Of the relation of the experiences which Christ had to His divine
nature he treats at some length in the third Oration

[1] *De Incarn.* 9.   [2] *Or.* I, 28.   [3] *Ibid.* II, 34.
[4] See *De Synodis*, 16.

against the Arians[1], and in one important passage we
may note the suggestion of the kind of link between
πάθος and sin, which we have already observed in
Gregory's reply to Eunomius. Athanasius says, "Let
no one then stumble at what belongs to man, but rather
let a man know that in nature the Word Himself is impassible, and yet, because of that flesh which He put on,
these things are ascribed to Him, since they are proper
to the flesh, and the body itself is proper to the Saviour.
And while He Himself being impassible in nature, remains as He is, not harmed by these affections[2], but
rather obliterating and destroying them, men, their passions as if changed and abolished in the Impassible,
henceforth become themselves also impassible and free
from them for ever, as John taught, saying, 'And ye
know that He was manifested to take away our sins, and
in Him is no sin.'" The same idea of the interchange between the passibility which Christ assumed through His
body and the impassibility which thereby He confers
upon men reappears in the letter to Epictetus: "for what
the human body of the Word suffered, this the Word,
dwelling in the body, ascribed to Himself, in order that
we might be enabled to be partakers of the Godhead of
the Word....And while He, the incorporeal, was in
the passible body, the body had in it the impassible Word,
which was destroying the infirmities inherent in the
body. But this He did, and so it was, in order that Himself taking what was ours and offering it as a sacrifice,
He might do away with it, and conversely might invest
us with what was His, and cause the Apostle to say:

[1] *Or.* III, 32–4.   [2] ἀπὸ τούτων.

'This corruptible must put on incorruption, and this mortal put on immortality[1].'"

In connexion with the confessions of faith which were so common in the fourth century, the formula of the Sirmium Synod of 357, known as the *Blasphemy*, may be referred to for the distinction which it suggests as constituting one of the elements in the Father's preeminence as compared with the Son. Among the characteristics of the Father is His impassibility. It is not said in the corresponding clause concerning the Son that He is passible, but later on the Scriptures are appealed to as teaching that He took from the Virgin Mary the manhood (*hominem*) through which He suffered. The word in Hilary's Latin is *compassus est*, and Phoebadius of Agen condemned the word in his comments on the formula, as implying the absence in Christ of the truly divine impassible *Spiritus*[2]. For the Arians there was no problem arising out of a union in Christ of the impassible and the passible, since for them the Son of God, preexistent but not eternal, who had taken to Himself flesh, was not essentially divine and therefore not essentially impassible. So Gregory of Nazianzus, writing to Cledonius, says that the Arians exclude the soul from

---

[1] *Ad Epict.* 6. The question, recently raised again by Dr Raven in his *Apollinarianism* as to what Athanasius meant when he spoke of Christ's experiences in the flesh, and whether he made room for the presence of a human soul in Christ, is one which I feel justified in leaving undiscussed. Athanasius recognized impassibility and passibility in Christ, however he explained the latter.

[2] Newman, *Athanasius*, i, p. 116, ii, p. 306. See Hahn, *Bibliothek*[3], pp. 199–201, for the Sirmian formula.

Christ's manhood, "that they may attribute His Passion to the Godhead, as that which gives motion to the body is also that which suffers[1]." For Gregory the antithesis "passible in His flesh, impassible in His Godhead" is one of a number of similar antitheses which necessarily result from the union of man and God in one Person.

The progress of Christological controversy led to differences in connexion with the passibility of the Incarnate Christ becoming more clear-cut, while they all stand out against a background of conviction that the Godhead, in and for itself, is impassible. The Two Natures doctrine gave the conditions for a precise ascription of passibility to the Lord's manhood, while, through what was to become the technical expression of the *communicatio idiomatum*, the Divine Person could be spoken of as truly the subject of the human experiences. The *Dogmatic Letter* of Cyril of Alexandria, and, with characteristic Western precision which owes much to Tertullian, the *Tome* of Leo, involve the same conclusion though the writers were moved by different religious interests, so far as Christology was their theme. But one interest they shared, that of showing that during the Incarnation the nature of the Godhead remained impassible. And to this those whom they respectively opposed were not less attached than them-

[1] *Ep.* 101; cf. Tixeront, *Histoire des Dogmes*, ii, p. 27, "if the Word is in Himself passible and subject to change, He can hold the place and perform the function of the soul in the body, and it then becomes proper to ascribe to Him the feelings and weaknesses attributed by Scripture to the humanity of Jesus."

selves. However the Christology of Theodore and Nestorius be interpreted, there can be no doubt that one of their original motives, and one of the causes of the aversion of Antiochenes like Nestorius and Theodoret from Cyril's teaching, was the conviction of the gulf dividing divine and human οὐσία, and the fear lest Cyril should be involving the very Godhead in all the experiences and weaknesses of human nature. Gregory of Nyssa had censured the adherents of Apollinarius because "they make the Deity of the Son mortal[1]." Nestorius, writing during exile in his own defence, makes it clear that what he dreaded in Cyril was doctrine which did not preserve distinct the properties of Godhead and manhood. Statements of Cyril, he says, "are really like those of Arius, since inconsistently with the *Ousia* of God, he attributed all the human things to the nature of God the Word through a union of *hypostasis* (*q'nômâ*), as though He (the Word) should suffer all human passions by physical sensation[2]." He himself while seeing in the Incarnation such a union of man and God "that in all things that which was by suffering and by its nature man should be a party to all the Divine things, and even impassibility[3]," maintains the strict differentiation of the natures. The manhood can be said to have been brought "into an appropriation with His own image," but not "into the *nature* of the in-

[1] Quoted by R. H. Baynes in a note on Hooker, Book v, 53, where Hooker himself attributes to Apollinarius the idea of a passible Deity.
[2] In Bethune-Baker, *Nestorius and his Teaching*, p. 160.
[3] *Ibid.* p. 132.

vincible and impassible *Ousia* of the Godhead[1]." The Antiochene position is to be found stated at length in the third of the dialogues which make up the *Eranistes*—a work of Theodoret's in which the controversy is developed in dialogue form. Theodoret had previously touched on the problem of the passibility of the Incarnate Christ in his reply, which was made in 431, to Cyril's twelve anathemas. In the twelfth, Cyril had condemned any denial of the fact that God the Word had tasted death in the flesh. Theodoret answers, "Passion is proper to the passible; the impassible is above passions. It was then the form of the servant that suffered, the form of God of course dwelling with it, and permitting it to suffer on account of the salvation brought forth of the sufferings, and making the sufferings its own on account of the union. Therefore it was not the Christ who suffered, but the man assumed of us by God[2]." In the dialogue, Eranistes commits himself at first to the position that God underwent the passion, and that the reason of the Incarnation was "that the impassible might undergo the passion by means of the passible." Orthodoxus refuses to accept terminology of this kind, or any assertion that God the Word tasted death, nor will he allow that the Word "shared" death. Eranistes defends himself by emphasizing the voluntary character of the passion; we ought to praise "the immensity of His love to man. For He suffered because He willed to suffer, and shared death because He wished it." But his

---

[1] *Nestorius and his Teaching*, pp. 138–9.
[2] In *Nicene and Post-Nicene Fathers*, vol. III, p. 31. "The Christ" means the Eternal Son.

opponent urges that God "wishes nothing inconsistent with His own nature," that in virtue of that nature certain things are impossible to God, and asks how, since this is admitted, it can be maintained that "His immortality and impassibility alone are subject to change." Eranistes pleads the language of Scripture and is answered by a reminder of the truth of the Two Natures, which leads to the conclusion that "as man He underwent the passion, as God He remained impassible." "How then," asks the other, "does the divine Scripture say that the Son of God suffered?" "Because," says Orthodoxus in language which recalls Cyril's *Dogmatic Letter*, "the body which suffered was His body." Eranistes, however, is still unsatisfied, and shortly returns to his contention that the Incarnation had made a real difference to God, since while He is "impassible and free from all want," yet, "after the Incarnation He became capable of suffering." Arguments as to the meaning of Biblical language and passages follow. Orthodoxus points out that in Scripture "the passion is never connected with the name 'God.'" Eranistes answers "But even I do not affirm that God the Word suffered apart from a body, but say that He suffered in flesh." This, however, is not accepted as legitimate: "you affirm then a mode of passion, not impassibility." And Orthodoxus appeals again to the analogy of soul and body; the soul does not die when the body dies, *a fortiori* the soul of the Saviour did not taste death, and, still more clearly, God the Word did not undergo the passion. "We say," rejoins Eranistes, "that He underwent the passion impassibly," and is ridiculed for the paradox. Orthodoxus will allow that the Lord's soul shared in suffering with the body, but not death; the Godhead shared neither. The argument continues to revolve round various scriptural texts, among which special attention is given to St Paul's words "had they known it, they would not have crucified the Lord of glory." Orthodoxus presses the doctrine of the Two Natures and of the *Communicatio idiomatum*, and as against any ascription of the passion to the Word appeals to passages from a number of the Fathers, including Irenaeus, Eustathius of Antioch, Athanasius, Gregory of Nyssa and John Chrysostom. Finally, in order that Eranistes may see that even well-known heretics have repudiated the doctrine of a passible divine nature, Apollinarius and Eusebius of Emesa are introduced. It is particularly interesting to note that Theodoret obviously did not regard the theology of Apollinarius as involving any such doctrine; on the occasions when he refers to him he makes no such charge, which one can hardly doubt that he would have done had he held it to be true[1]. In this dialogue Orthodoxus gives a sentence from the *Tract concerning the Faith*: "Since the passions are concerned with the flesh His power possessed its own impassibility, so to refer the passion to the power is an impious error." The quotation from Eusebius shows a remarkable variation from what would be expected of one whom Jerome could call

[1] In *Ep.* 180, written to Domnus of Antioch on Cyril's death, Theodoret makes special reference to Cyril's false teaching (as he interpreted it) on this point "investing an immortal nature with death." But the shades below will not stand it, even Pharaoh and Sennacherib will join in stoning him.

signifer Arianae factionis, in its strong repudiation of suffering in connexion with the Son of God, "the Power which was before the ages by nature incorporeal, in dignity impassible." But the whole passage is quite free from Arianism.

So the dialogue ends with Orthodoxus the victor. And as Eranistes could never challenge the doctrine that the Godhead is in and for itself impassible, nor refuse to acknowledge the two natures in Christ, there could be no other result. Theodoret says in the dialogue hardly anything that could be interpreted as implying "two persons in Christ." In so far as Antiochene theologians ever did take up that position, the passibility of the human nature in Christ would be the passibility of a man Jesus. That is in itself intelligible enough. It is when we pass to the extreme developments on the other side that the whole question of the sufferings of the Incarnate Christ becomes much more complicated. That arises out of the way in which the union of the divine and the human in Christ was construed, and especially out of the idea of the deification of His human nature. Neither the Christology of Apollinarius nor that of Cyril forces the consideration of this notion to the front. Dr Raven's account of the Christology of Apollinarius leads to a clear understanding of the difference between him and the later Monophysites. One might express it by saying that with them the outstanding fact is the deification of the human, with him the Kenosis of the divine. In a confession of faith of an Apollinarian synod which Dr Raven thinks may be "the last writing of the Bishop of Laodicea," anathema is pronounced on anyone "who denies that the flesh is from Mary and says that it is of the uncreated nature and consubstantial with God": and also on him "who says that the Godhead is passible and that the sufferings which come from the soul come from it[1]." As for Cyril, he makes it sufficiently clear in the third letter to Nestorius that he taught neither "a conversion of the flesh into the nature of Deity nor a change of the ineffable substance of God the Word into the substance of the flesh," and that while the Son of God "exists in His own nature impassible," He was "in the crucified body making the sufferings of His own flesh His own in an impassible manner." Similar language is used in the letter to John of Antioch: "*Let the heavens rejoice.*" I think that the two facts, directly relevant in this connexion as points in Cyril's teaching, that the Word is in His own nature impassible and that the sufferings of the flesh are natural to the flesh, even though it is the flesh of the Word[2], need to be remembered by the reader of Harnack's pages on the Christology of Cyril. Harnack suggests that Cyril's doctrine is one of the deification of Christ's humanity, when he interprets Cyril's formula as to the one nature after the

[1] *Apollinarianism*, pp. 218–19; cf. p. 220. "Any doctrine which merges the human in the divine, such as is to be found in the true Monophysites, would render meaningless his emphasis upon the self-limitation of the Son of God, and upon the transference of attributes, both of which are introduced in order to guard against such confusion while preserving the real union."

[2] Cf. the quotation from the letter to Successus in Loofs' *Leitfaden*[4], p. 292: "Two natures came together with one another in an indissoluble union, without confusion and without change; for the flesh is flesh and not Deity even though it has become the flesh of God."

Incarnation (μία φύσις τοῦ θεοῦ λόγου σεσαρκω-
μένη) as transferring the humanity "entirely to the
substance of the God Logos[1]." But if this were the
case, suffering would no longer be proper to the flesh,
and the reality of the passion would need to be explained,
as later in Monophysitism, in some other way than by
treating it as an experience which is proper to humanity.

For in Monophysitism it became necessary to show
how the Incarnate Christ could suffer at all. This was a
problem, even though not realized as such, from the
moment Eutyches, having been questioned by com-
missioners sent to him from the Constantinopolitan
synod of 448, affirmed that, though Christ was true God
and true man, His body was not consubstantial with
ours[2]. From this position he was, with obvious reluct-
ance, prepared later to withdraw, but it was involved in
the character of his Christology. The more Eutyches
refused to allow the co-existence of the two natures
after the Incarnation, the more certain it was that a
doctrine of the passibility of the Godhead would be
attributed to him. Accordingly, there is nothing surprising in the fact that the Council of Chalcedon in its
Definition refers expressly to this point, condemning
those who "foolishly imagine that there is one nature of
the flesh and of the Godhead," and "monstrously suppose that by reason of the confusion (συγχύσει) the
divine nature of the Only begotten is passible." It is a
matter of minor importance whether Eutyches taught a

[1] *Hist. Dogm.* IV, p. 177.
[2] Hefele, *History of the Christian Councils*, III, p. 192
(Eng. tr.).

mixture or confusion of the natures, or, rather a trans-
mutation, through the union, of the nature of humanity
into the nature of deity. The doctrinal history of the
East during the next hundred years shows the strength
of the tendency towards such a deification of the humanity which was unified with the Godhead that the
idea of divine impassibility falls into the background.
The divisions within Monophysitism need not be
treated at length. Zeno's *Henoticon* of 483, by its
silence on the question of whether in Christ there are
two natures or one, was, for all its reconciling intention,
an opener-up of fresh controversy, since it did not uphold
the terminology of Chalcedon, and could, by its reference
to Chalcedon, as a place where heretical opinions
might have been held, be interpreted as slighting the
conclusions of the Fourth Council. Still, when it asserts
that to One Person belong both the miracles and the
sufferings "which He voluntarily underwent in the
flesh" it says nothing to which the most whole-hearted
supporter of the Chalcedonian Definition need have
taken exception. It is otherwise with such men as Peter
Fullo, monophysite Bishop of Antioch, and Julian of
Halicarnassus, and with their expressions of doctrine.
It was Peter who about the year 470 added to the Tris-
hagion the words "Holy God, Holy Strong One, Holy
Immortal One, Who was crucified for our sake, have
mercy upon us." This formula, open as it was to grave
objection for its bearing on Trinitarian theology, did not
secure dogmatic sanction. The nearest approach to it is
the anathema of the Fifth General Council of 553 pronounced on anyone "who does not confess that our

Lord Jesus Christ who was crucified in the flesh is true God and Lord of glory and One of the Holy Trinity." The positive formula, thus justified by the Council, was championed about the year 518 by certain Scythian monks. Harnack says their "soundness in the faith was unimpeachable[1]." It is not Theopaschite in any other sense than is the old tradition of speech which allows of such expressions as "the sufferings of God" or "the Son of God was crucified," while, in respect of the doctrine of the Trinity, it is quite successful, as Peter's liturgical addition is not, in avoiding any semblance of Sabellianism without, on the other hand, deviating into Tritheism. An extreme point in Monophysitism was reached by Julian of Halicarnassus and his supporters. Dorner thus describes their position: they "developed the propositions laid down by Eutyches and Dioscorus, and maintained that the humanity of Christ according to the $\phi\acute{v}\sigma\iota\varsigma$ which pertained to it subsequently to the Unio could not be said to be susceptible of human weaknesses and sufferings; and that, on the contrary, the body of Christ, equally with the Godhead, was in itself, or by its very nature, raised above even innocent physical need and weaknesses ($\pi\acute{a}\theta\eta$ $\dot{a}\delta\iota\acute{a}\beta\lambda\eta\tau a$). It was $\ddot{a}\phi\theta a\rho\tau o\varsigma$ and was of the same nature as the body of Adam before the fall, which also would never have died, had not Adam sinned. In asserting the supernatural character of the body of Christ they did not intend to deny its actual reality; they did, however, aim at giving greater prominence to the love of Christ, by tracing, not merely the sufferings themselves, but even the possibility of

[1] *Hist. Dogm.* IV, p. 230.

suffering to a free act of love, by which Christ renounced the impassibility which previously characterized His body, and undertook both our capability of suffering and the sufferings themselves[1]." Their opponents within the borders of Monophysitism, who followed Severus of Antioch in affirming that the body of Christ was consubstantial with our bodies, and could not be regarded as impassible and incorruptible in its οὐσία, gave them the nick-name Aphthartodoketists, and were in turn attacked as Phthartolatrists. And on both sides there were further developments.

Behind the formulae and the dialectic of Monophysitism a religious motive can be descried. That is the interest in soteriology and the conviction that redemption is possible only if He who has suffered and died is truly divine. The saying of Apollinarius, "the death of a man does not annul death," is a clear expression of this interest. On the other hand, belief in the impassibility of the Godhead was a matter of formal doctrine rather than of vital concern. It stood in no direct relation to soteriology. Theodoret and the Antiochene School in general were interested in it because it was a notable element in safeguarding the absolute distinction between the οὐσίαι of Godhead and manhood. Whenever the doctrine of the Two Natures was abandoned, or if the differentiation of the Natures was conceived of as theoretical only, the absoluteness of the distinction just mentioned was endangered. Such a formula as "One nature, but incarnate and made man," which Flavian of Constantinople, in a confession of his faith of the year 448,

[1] *Doctrine of the Person of Christ*, Div. II, vol. I, p. 129.

says "We do not refuse to affirm[1]" (he had already expressed his belief in the Two Natures), does not escape that danger. And when we come to the Julianists among the Monophysites, the distinction, within the Incarnation, has vanished; for, on the one hand, the human nature is so deified from the moment of its union with the divine, that the divine properties, such as impassibility and incorruptibility, become its properties; on the other, it is an act of pure grace on the part of the Word which allows the body to experience sufferings, since apart from such grace suffering could not touch it. This reminds us of Eranistes in Theodoret's Dialogue arguing that the Word suffered out of His love of man, and because He willed to suffer. It is the religious interest visible in Monophysitism which gives it an appeal to one's sympathy which, in its purely intellectual aspects, it lacks. In his work *The Progress of Dogma*, Dr James Orr says of the mode of thinking which we connect with Alexandrine theology and with the Monophysite point of view, that in it "there was the ineradicable conviction that, however the union of the divine and human in the Person of Jesus was to be conceived, it was something infinitely richer, more vital and penetrative, than the Chalcedonian formulation took account of[2]." The Monophysites do, at least, secure the belief that the Incarnation and all its experiences had a meaning for the Eternal Word, which it is not so easy to secure if the emphasis is laid on the human nature in distinction from the divine, rather than on the One

---

[1] Hahn, *Bibliothek*, p. 321.
[2] Orr, *Progress of Dogma*, p. 193.

Person, whose are all the experiences which form the content of the incarnate life.

Greek theology reached its orthodox culmination in the work of John of Damascus, after Leontius of Byzantium by his doctrine of the *Enhypostasia* had found a way of expressing the truth that a φύσις must have its πρόσωπον, a point of importance in connexion with the Nestorian controversy[1]. At the outset of his *Exposition of the Orthodox Faith,* John relates the passionlessness of the divine nature to the fact that "God, being good, is the cause of all good, subject neither to envy nor to any passion[2]," thus supplying an ethical basis for a metaphysical truth. This impassibility is, however, possible only because God is incorporeal, "simple and not compound[3]," and, this being so, we can understand how it is that God "is not subject to passion or flux either in begetting or in creating[4]." The anthropomorphic language of Scripture with reference to bodily parts in God is explained as symbolical and conformed to human weakness of understanding, with the exception of what concerns "the bodily sojourn of the God-Word. For He for our safety took upon Himself the whole nature of man, the thinking spirit, the body, and all the properties of human nature, even the natural and blameless passions[5]." In the second book, the twenty-second chapter is, in part, devoted to a discussion of passion, a word which, as used of the body, "refers to diseases and

[1] On the difficulties attaching to the use of the word πρόσωπον, in the singular and in the plural, particularly as used by Nestorius, see Loofs' *Nestorius,* pp. 75–94.

[2] *Exposition,* i, 1 (*Nicene and Post-Nicene Fathers,* vol. ix).

[3] *Ibid.* i, 4.   [4] *Ibid.* i, 8.   [5] *Ibid.* i, 11.

wounds," as used of the soul "means desire and anger."
"But to speak broadly and generally, passion is an animal
affection which is succeeded by pleasure and pain." A
further definition is given of passions of the soul: "passion is a sensible activity of the appetitive faculty, de-
pending on the presentation to the mind of something
good or bad. For the notion of something good results
in desire, and the notion of something bad results in
anger. But passion considered as a class, that is, passion
in general, is defined as a movement in one thing caused
by another. Energy, on the other hand, is a drastic
movement, and by 'drastic' is meant that which is
moved of itself." This idea of passion, and contrast of
it with energy, though energy may be called a passion
when its action is not in accordance with nature, is of
great importance in its bearing on the notion of the divine impassibility. If passion is a "movement at variance
with nature," to ascribe passion to God would mean
that He, under the influence of some cause external to
Himself, became the subject of an experience to which
His nature was opposed. But such an introduction of
the idea of constraint would involve a reconsideration of
theistic philosophy precisely at the point where the distinction between God and the world seems clearest. In
the third book, which deals with the Incarnation, the
distinctness of the two natures is set forth, the impassibility of the divine nature is emphasized, the human experiences, which include the endurance of the "natural
and innocent passions[1]," are conceived of as resulting
from the "permission of the divine will[2]," while the

[1] *Exposition*, III, 18.   [2] *Ibid.*

deification of the flesh does not mean that the flesh was "changed in its own nature or in its natural properties[1]." Accordingly, we may say that for John the passions were in Christ the result both of the fact of the reality of His manhood and of the willingness of the Word that the flesh should suffer what was proper to it; "for no compulsion is contemplated in Him but all is voluntary. For it was with His will that He hungered and thirsted and feared and died[2]." The human activity is called passion "because it is moved," but the character of the passion is explained in terms of soteriology. He "assumed all the natural and innocent passions of man," and with the purpose "that He might sanctify all[3]." As to the impassibility of the Word in respect of the divine nature, the treatment of this subject in the first part of the chapter specially devoted to it may be quoted: "the Word of God then itself endured all in the flesh while His divine nature which alone was passionless remained void of passion. For since the one Christ who is a compound of divinity and humanity and exists in divinity and humanity, truly suffered, that part which is capable of passion suffered as it was natural it should, but that part which was void of passion did not share in the suffering. For the soul, indeed, since it is capable of passion shares in the pain and suffering of a bodily cut, though it is not cut itself, but only the body: but the divine part which is void of passion does not share in the suffering of the body[4]."

John of Damascus held that Christ in His human

---

[1] *Exposition*, III, 17.   [2] *Ibid.* III, 20.
[3] *Ibid.*   [4] *Ibid.* III, 26.

nature had true experience of suffering. He assumed the "natural and innocent" passions both of the body and the mind. As to the latter, he discusses Christ's experience of fear and decides that He "willingly and spontaneously accepted that which was not natural. So that fear itself and terror and agony belong to the natural and innocent passions and are not under the dominion of sin[1]."

Very different had been the teaching of Hilary of Poitiers, to which we may now turn. Hilary presses the idea of impassibility to a point where the exemplary value of Christ's experiences in His human nature almost completely disappears. It is in the tenth book of his work *De Trinitate* that we obtain a full account of his doctrine. The Incarnation means that "the Man Jesus Christ, Only-begotten God, as flesh and as Word, at the same time Son of Man and Son of God, without ceasing to be Himself, that is, God, took true humanity after the likeness of our humanity." Then he passes to the characteristic feature in his conception of the Lord's human nature: "When, in this humanity, He was struck with blows, or smitten with wounds, or bound with ropes, or lifted on high, He felt the force of suffering, but without its pain"..."He had a body to suffer, and he suffered: but He had not a nature which could feel pain. For His body possessed a unique nature of its own[2]." Hilary thinks of Christ as never needing to satisfy bodily longings. Very curiously he remarks, "it is never said that the Lord ate or drank or wept when He was hungry or thirsty or sorrowful. He conformed to the habits of the body to prove the reality of His own

[1] *Exposition*, III, 23.   [2] *De Trinitate*, x, 23.

body, to satisfy the custom of human bodies by doing as our nature does. When he ate and drank, it was a concession, not to His own necessities, but to our habits[1]."

He argues from *a priori* considerations that One who had the power to heal and restore would not Himself be subject to pain, and his general explanation of Gospel texts which could be urged against him is that Christ spoke with a view to the needs of others, not to His own. The following passage gives us a compendium of Hilary's conclusions: "it is then a mistaken opinion of human judgment, which thinks He felt pain because He suffered. He bore our sins, that is, He assumed our body of sin, but was Himself sinless. He was sent in the likeness of the flesh of sin, bearing sin indeed in His flesh, but *our* sin. So too He felt pain for us, but not with our senses; He was found in fashion as a man, with a body which could feel pain, but His nature could not feel pain; for, though His fashion was that of a man, His origin was not human, but He was born by conception of the Holy Ghost[2]." The same attitude appears in his commentary on the fifty-fourth psalm. Whether this Christology should be spoken of as "indisputably docetic[3]" depends on the meaning or meanings attached to the adjective in question, but it certainly evacuates the Pas-

---

[1] *De Trinitate*, x, 24.   [2] *Ibid.* x, 47.

[3] Raven, *Apollinarianism*, 96. Dr Raven says this is admitted. In the *Nicene and Post-Nicene Fathers*, vol. ix, p. lxxvii, it is said "Hilary has been accused of 'sailing somewhat close to the cliffs of Docetism,' but all admit that he has escaped shipwreck." The editors obviously felt embarrassed by Hilary's standpoint. They say what they can for him, but in the end it does not amount to very much.

sion narratives in the Gospels of their force and appeal to man. Suffering undertaken for the sake of men, yet without pain, is not the suffering which has drawn men to the Cross of Christ.

5. FROM AUGUSTINE TO THE SCHOLASTICS

When we come to the greatest of the Western Fathers we find attention given in a number of his works to elements inherent in the general subject of the divine impassibility. Reference may be made, first of all, to Augustine's account of the meaning of *passio*. He says of it that it is derived from πάθος and means "a movement of the mind contrary to reason[1]," and so naturally concludes that it is incompatible with blessedness. At the same time, passions such as anger and sadness can be turned to purposes of righteousness (*in usus iustitiae*). Man's life does not become blessed by the cessation of movement in it, but "this is a blessed and peaceful life of man when all its movements agree with reason and truth; then they are called joys and holy affections, pure and good. But if they do not agree, they tear the soul apart and make life most wretched, and are called perturbations and lusts and evil desires[2]." The blessedness of Adam before the Fall lay in the fact that his life was free from fear and pain[3].

It is in the freedom from all disturbance, from all the weaknesses and defects which in human experience are associated with the various phases of the emotional life, that Augustine sees the divine impassibility, while he

[1] *De Civ. Dei*, VIII, 17.   [2] *De Gen. cont. Manich.* I, 20.
[3] *De Civ. Dei*, XIV, 10.

aims at doing justice to what is said in the Bible concerning the feelings and corresponding actions of God. As to the scriptural expressions he regards them as the best manner of speech possible, in view of the necessary limitations of language when any attempt is made to describe the life of God. So, as God is said to have a soul only by analogy (*tropice*)[1], we must think of justice and similar qualities as attributed to God because nothing better can be said; such terms are used because of human infirmity[2]. And, further, we must remember that when any emotion is ascribed to God, that is not to be understood as implying changeableness in God or any disturbance (*perturbatio*) within His life. Augustine's meaning may be illustrated from his treatment of God's "repentance" and "anger." Thus, as to the former, repentance is to be understood as existing after an ineffable manner, and while Scripture everywhere witnesses that God is pitiful, this emotion differs from human pity which brings "some misery of heart," and "who can sanely say that God is touched by any misery[3]?" In the next section of the same treatise he says "with regard to pity, if you take away the compassion which involves a sharing of misery with him whom you pity, so that there remains the peaceful goodness of helping and freeing from misery, some kind of knowledge of the divine pity is suggested." Elsewhere he affirms that God's repentance involves no change in His plans, since God's mercy is given in answer to the prayers He foreknew[4]. So God

---

[1] *De Civ. Dei*, XVI, 53.   [2] *Serm.* CCCXLI, 7.
[3] *De div. quaest. ad Simpl.* II, 2.
[4] *Enarr. in Ps.* CV, 35.

does not suffer the pain of repentance like man, but "when He changes His works because of His unchangeable counsel, on account of that very change, not of the counsel, but of the work, He is said to repent[1]." As to God's anger, that is interpreted by Augustine as expressing God's judicial punishment of sin. That punishment (*vindicta*) takes place "without any perturbation of mind[2]." From any such emotional or mental disturbance God the judge is free, "but what happens in His ministers, because it happens through His laws, is called His anger[3]."

A passage of some length may be quoted in which Augustine makes his whole point of view clear: "God," he says, "does not repent as does a man, but as God; just as He is not angry after the manner of men, nor is pitiful, nor is jealous, but all He is He is as God. God's repentance does not follow upon error; the anger of God carries with it no trace[4] of a disturbed mind, nor His pity the wretched heart of a fellow-sufferer,...nor His jealousy any envy of mind. But by the repentance of God is meant the change of things which lie within His power, unexpected by man; the anger of God is His vengeance upon sin; the pity of God is the goodness of His help; the jealousy of God is that providence whereby He does not allow those whom He has in subjection to Himself to love with impunity what He forbids." The conclusion is that "when God repents He is not changed and He brings about change; when He is angry He is not moved and He avenges; when He pities He does not

[1] *Enarr. in Ps.* cxxxi, 18.   [2] *De div. quaest.* i, 52.
[3] *Enarr. in Ps.* vi, 3.   [4] Literally "heart."

grieve and He liberates; when He is jealous He is not pained and He causes pain[1]."

In the treatise *On Patience* there is another relevant statement of the contrast between fact and feeling as conceived of by Augustine in relation to the divine life: "Patience is spoken of as belonging even to God. So though God can suffer nothing, while patience takes its name from suffering, nevertheless we not only faithfully believe, but also healthfully confess, that God is patient. But of what kind and how great the patience of God is who can explain, when we speak of Him as suffering nothing, yet not as without patience, but rather as most patient? His patience is therefore ineffable, even as His jealousy, His anger, and any other similar characteristics. For if we think of them as though they were ours, none such exist in Him. For none of them do we experience without vexation, but far be it from us to imagine that the impassible nature of God suffers any vexation. For as He is jealous without any envy, is angry without any perturbation, is pitiful without any grief, repents without having any evil in Him to correct, so He is patient without any suffering[2]."

While Augustine differentiates in respect of human life between *passiones*, according as they do or do not allow of being used to a good end, the ideal which he sees as finally possible for man, though not under the conditions of earthly life, is a state of ἀπάθεια, involving a nearer approach of the human nature to the divine. In God there is "no defect, no need, no necessity[3]," but

[1] *Cont. adv. leg. et prophet.* i, 40.　　[2] *De Patientia*, i.
[3] *De div. quaest.* LXXXIII, 22.

of men "even when we have our affections right and according to God, they belong to this life not to that which we hope will be, and often we yield to them even unwillingly. We have them owing to the weakness of our human state, not so the Lord Jesus whose weakness sprang from power[1]." Augustine's conception of the meaning of impassibility is given in a passage of his work *On the City of God*. "That which in Greek is called ἀπάθεια, which would be called *impassibilitas*, if it could be expressed in Latin, understood in the following manner (with reference to the mind not to the body), as a life without those feelings which take place contrary to reason and disturb the mind, is clearly good and greatly to be desired: but it does not belong to this life." Augustine appeals to 1 St John i, 8 as to universal sin, and continues, "and so ἀπάθεια will then exist when there shall be no sin in man. . . . Further, if by that ἀπάθεια is meant a condition when no feeling can in any way touch the mind, who would not judge this insensibility to be worse than all vices? It can therefore not unreasonably be said that perfect blessedness will exist without sting of fear and without sadness; who will have said that there will not be there love and joy, unless he be in every way shut off from truth? But if ἀπάθεια means a condition where no fear terrifies and pain does not vex us, it is to be avoided in this life if we wish to live rightly, that is according to God; but in that blessed life which is promised as eternal it is clearly to be the object of our hope[2]." What emerges from this survey of Augustine's thought is the difficulty of combining in a real unity what

[1] *De Civ. Dei*, XIV, 4.   [2] *Ibid.* XIV, 8. 4.

are known as the metaphysical and the moral attributes of God. On the one hand there is the self-sufficiency of the divine nature, its absolute transcendence, its imperviousness to all assault, so that, in Augustine's words, "no one can hurt the nature of God[1]"; on the other hand, it is impossible not to ascribe to God certain ethical attitudes and outgoings of His will towards the world which in our case are properly describable as anger, repentance, pity, and so on. That Augustine intends to preserve the double reality is the conclusion naturally to be drawn from his various statements; it is less easy to be convinced of his success, though the theistic philosopher will agree with what underlies much of his argument, namely that God has perfect control of His feelings in a way which lies beyond human experience, and is never surprised into any kind of involuntary outpouring of this or that emotion.

The results which follow in connexion with the idea of the *passio* of God, when the doctrine of God is handled from the standpoint of a wholly transcendental philosophy and by methods of rigorously logical procedure, can be studied in the work *De Divisione Naturae* of the ninth century theologian John Scotus Erigena. The end of the first book is taken up with a discussion between the Disciple and the Master concerning the last two categories, those of action and of being acted upon[2]. The main content of the passage is the effort and success of the Master in satisfying the Disciple that, since what is said of God, whether in respect of words of active or of passive significance, is said of Him not with exactness but

[1] *De nat. bon. cont. Manich.* 1, 40.   [2] *Patiendi.*

metaphorically, "in truth God neither acts nor is acted upon, neither moves nor is moved, neither loves nor is loved[1]." It is not surprising that the Disciple is, at first, bewildered by a conclusion so contrary to what seems to him to be given in the authoritative sources of Scripture and the Fathers. Into the subtleties of the argument and the question of substance and accidents as applied to God it is not necessary to go. Agreement is reached as to the impossibility of supposing that anything can be regarded as an accident of the divine nature, or that the divine nature can be an accident of anything, "otherwise it would seem to be passible, changeable and capable of (assuming) another nature[2]." Accordingly, as to act and to be acted upon are accidents, they are not applicable to God. The Master has still to offer much explanation before the Disciple is satisfied as to the inapplicability of action to God; he is, as indeed we should expect, more readily convinced on the other side: "concerning the passive (*pati*) I could in no way doubt, for that God is altogether impassible I both believe and understand; that passive estate (*passionem*) I mean which is opposed to action, that is, being acted upon. For who will have said or believed, not to speak of understanding, that God can be passively affected (*pati*), seeing that He is the Creator, not a creature[3]?" The more difficult problem is solved through the recognition of the unity of being and action in God, so that no place is to be found, where the divine nature is concerned, for a category of action; the Dis-

---

[1] *De Div. Nat.* p. 504, sec. 62 B.
[2] *Ibid.* p. 508, sec. 68 B.
[3] *Ibid.* p. 516, sec. 71 B.

ciple allows, with no further delay, that no category can apply to God[1]. The book ends with the settlement by the Master of the Disciple's doubts on the subject of love. God is to be conceived of as love, "because He is the cause of all love, and is diffused through all things, and gathers all things into one, and comes back to Himself in an ineffable return, and brings to an end in Himself the loving movements of every creature." God is said to be loved by all things which proceed from Him, "not because He, who alone is impassible, becomes, in respect of them, the subject of any kind of passivity, but because all things seek Him and His beauty draws all things to Himself[2]."

It is not I think doubtful that the kind of understanding of God which may be won from these pages of John Scotus is one that must, despite all the dialectical subtlety with which it is fortified, be in permanent difficulties with the New Testament. What it is immediately relevant to point out is that a certain line in theistic argument or in philosophy of religion, if developed exclusively and pressed far enough, leads to a point where every distinct quality and attribute disappears from the divine nature. That would be too high a price to pay for preserving the notion of impassibility. At the same time, I am not assuming that it is necessary to pay it.

With Anselm we are on the verge of the great scholastic movement. He devotes a short chapter of the *Proslogion* to the resolving of the paradox presented by

[1] "Nunc nullam categoriam in Deum cadere incunctanter intelligo." *De Div. Nat.* p. 518, sec. 72 B.

[2] *Ibid.* p. 519, sec. 74.

the combination of pity with impassibility in the divine life. It is one of many similar riddles. "How," asks Anselm, "art Thou at once pitiful and impassible? For if Thou art impassible, Thou dost not suffer with man; if Thou dost not suffer with man, Thy heart is not wretched by compassion with the wretched, which is the meaning of being pitiful. But if Thou art not pitiful, whence can the wretched gain so great comfort? How then art Thou, and art Thou not pitiful, Lord, except that Thou art pitiful in respect of us, and not in respect of Thyself? Truly Thou art so in respect of our feeling, and art not in respect of Thine. For when Thou lookest upon us in our wretchedness we feel the effect of Thy pity, Thou feelest not the effect. And therefore Thou art pitiful, because Thou savest the wretched, and sparest the sinners who belong to Thee; and Thou art not pitiful, because Thou art touched by no fellow-suffering in that wretchedness[1]." Thus pity is interpreted as a movement from God to man, of which movement man reaps the benefit; it is not a state which is found existing in God and involving on His part an experience analogous to that which must be ascribed to a wretched man. Elsewhere, in the *Cur Deus Homo*, Anselm affirms "without doubt" the impassibility of the divine nature, which cannot be brought down from its height. "Wherefore when we say that God suffers anything lowly or weak, we do not understand this in respect of the height of the impassible nature, but in respect of the weakness of the human substance which He wore[2]."

From Anselm we may pass to Aquinas with, perhaps,

[1] *Proslog.* 8.   [2] *Cur Deus Homo*, i, 8.

some regret that among the problems which Heloissa submitted to Abelard none touched on the question of the divine impassibility and of the reconciliation of that idea with expressions in Scripture which seem to point in the other direction. Nor has he left us anything on the subject in his formal expositions of the doctrine of God.

That Aquinas could not have admitted any possibility in God may be clearly understood from a comparison of his teaching as to the perfection of God with his analysis of the meaning of *passio*. In the divine perfection is involved the divine immutability; no one of the diverse possibilities of change which exist in the case of creatures can be conceived of as applicable to God[1]. Neither His knowledge[2] nor His will[3] admits of variation or change. *Passio*, on the contrary, involves precisely those ideas of change and contingency which the conception of God as "altogether simple[4]," as "pure activity[5]," as perfect and containing the perfection of all things[6], cannot admit. For *passio*, when the term is used exactly, means the abandonment of some natural quality and the impress of a quality foreign and adverse[7], and this could not be supposed as taking place in connexion with God. The notion of a *Deus passibilis* is incompatible with the definition of a primary being who must be "pure action without the admixture of any potentiality, because potentiality itself is later than action. Now everything which in any way is changed is in some way in a state of potentiality, whence it is

---

[1] *Summa Theologica*, I, qu. 9, art. 1–2.
[2] *Ibid.* I, 14. 15.   [3] *Ibid.* I, 19. 7.   [4] *Ibid.* I, 3. 7.
[5] *Ibid.* I, 9. 1.   [6] *Ibid.* I, 4. 1–2.   [7] *Ibid.* II A, 22. 1.

obvious that God cannot in any way be changed[1]." We may contrast the argument wherein Aquinas shows that the soul can suffer, since to suffer belongs to whatever exists in a state of potentiality, "and the soul though not composed of matter and form, yet possesses some measure of potentiality, in accordance with which it is possible for it to receive and to suffer[2]." The necessarily complete freedom of God from *passio* is made clearer by reference to the discussion of the meaning of *potentia* and of its admissibility as existing in God. *Potentia,* says Aquinas, is twofold, passive and active. As active it is supremely present in God, as the principle of action directed towards something: but the passive *potentia* is wholly absent from Him, for *passio* is to be attributed to something only in respect of its deficiencies and imperfections, and cannot have any place in God who is pure action, altogether perfect. The passive potentiality which is "the principle of being acted upon by something else" cannot exist in God[3].

The twentieth question of the First Part of the *Summa* shows us how Aquinas argues to the existence of love in God, without at the same time ascribing to God any *passio,* and distinguishes between love and joy which can be regarded as really existing in God, and sadness and anger which can be attributed to Him only by way of metaphor. Love, which has regard to the good absolutely and not under some particular condition, is "the first action of the will and the desire." Accordingly

---

[1] *Summa Theologica,* I, 9. I.   [2] *Ibid.* II A, 22. I.

[3] *Ibid.* I, 25. I, "principium patiendi ab alio." The Dominican translation is followed in the text.

love is the first root of every movement of desire. "For no one desires anything except a good which is loved; nor does anyone rejoice except over a good which is loved. Hate also does not exist except in respect of what is contrary to something loved. Similarly it is clear that sadness and the like are referred to love as to a first principle. Wherefore wherever there is will or desire, there love must exist. For if that which is original is taken away all else is taken away also. Now it has been demonstrated that in God there is will. And so love must be held to exist in Him." That love does not involve *passio* in God is shown by the distinction drawn between acts of desire in which the senses are involved, and acts of desire which concern the intellect alone. In the case of man "the intellectual desire, which is called the will, moves through the mediation of the desire which springs from the senses." Such desires which involve bodily change "are spoken of as passions, not as acts of the will. Love, therefore, and joy and delight, in so far as they signify acts of sense-desire, are passions, but not in so far as they signify acts of intellectual desire; and so they are held to exist in God. So the Philosopher says that 'God rejoices with an energy which is one and simple,' and after the same manner He loves without passion." Further, whereas anger and sadness imply the presence of some imperfection, and so can be ascribed to God only metaphorically, no such imperfection is included in love and joy: these, therefore, can properly be predicated of God, yet "without passion[1]." In his other chief work Aquinas devotes a chapter to a statement of what does

[1] *Summa Theologica*, I, 20. I.

not lie within the omnipotence of God and of the reasons for such limitations[1]. Whereas in man there is both active and passive potentiality, only the former can be ascribed to God. Passive potentiality has reference to being, as active potentiality to action. "Wherefore potentiality to being exists in those things alone which possess matter subject to contrariety. Since, therefore, passive potentiality does not exist in God, in whatsoever pertains to His own being God lacks potentiality[2]. God cannot, therefore, be a body or anything of that kind."

Further, the action of passive potentiality of this kind is movement. God, therefore, since passive potentiality has no place in Him, cannot be changed. Moreover, since deficiency is a sort of corruption, it follows that in nothing can He be deficient.

Again, every deficiency exists in respect of some want. But the subject of want is the potentiality of matter. In no way, therefore, can He be deficient. Further, since weariness exists through defect of power, and forgetfulness through defect of knowledge, it is obvious that He can neither be weary not forget. Moreover, He can neither be overcome nor suffer violence; for these things take place in respect of that which has a moveable nature.

And in the same way He cannot repent, nor be angry, nor sad, since all these things express imperfection and passion and defect.

With regard to the Incarnation Aquinas shows that it is true to say that Christ's soul was passible, both by

[1] *Summa contra Gentiles*, II, 25.
[2] This is another way of stating the absolute and immutable simplicity of the divine nature.

reason of its connexion with the passible body and because those feelings which are called passions of the soul were in Christ, though he notes three respects in which these passions were present in Christ in a manner different from their presence in men. This general position is worked out in detail in connexion with various particular passions[1].

Not less positive on the subject of the divine impassibility is Duns Scotus[2]. We may start from his affirmations that we may show what God is not by denying the applicability to Him of any composite character or motion, and that in God there can be no real distinction of accidents from Himself[3]. The position is reached that "the first principle, inasmuch as it is in itself the most perfect of all entities, existing necessarily of itself, in absolute simplicity, action separated from all matter and potentiality, neither in fact nor in reason is capable of undergoing any kind of change." Then, after the argument from motion to the unmoving has been set forth, he continues, "so it is proper that the first mover of all should be altogether motionless and unchangeable. Now that no change can take place in Him, since He has the characteristic of the formal cause, is shown by the fact that nothing at all can be acted upon[4], except through a material principle, just as it cannot act except through a formal principle; therefore it is impossible for the first form to be acted upon, unless it brings with it an element of materiality; but God is altogether immaterial;

---

[1] *Summa Theologica*, III, 15. 4 ff.
[2] The edition published at Rome in 1900 has been used.
[3] *Summa Theologica*, Pars I, Tom. I, Qu. 3.   [4] *pati.*

therefore as the first form He is altogether impassible and immutable[1]."

Later, he deals with the argument that an element of change may be found in God owing to the fact of creation as distinguished from God's eternal foreknowledge of creation. He replies that in respect of the divine mind no harmony can be established between any sort of potentiality and change and mutability and God, so that there is never any possibility of affirming any change in God.

In the nineteenth question he returns to the same thesis and conclusion on the inquiry "whether the will of God is changeable." The background of what seems like change, for example in God's dealings with Nineveh as recorded in the Book of Jonah, is eternal changelessness. If there seems to be a change in God's will, that is due to a change in earthly affairs; if in any case anything seems to happen contrary to God's laws, "it is certainly not as proceeding and arising from any change of will." Change and exceptions to universal law must be viewed against the background of God's eternal unchangeable will which makes room for certain events to take place for moral reasons[2].

One further reference to Duns Scotus may be made in connexion with his discussion of the divine *misericordia*. "There seems," he says, "not to be pity in God. For pity, according to John of Damascus, is compassion for the evils of others; but in God there is no compassion, since, if it were present, He would suffer some sadness: so pity has no place in Him." Yet there is pity in God,

[1] *Summa Theologica*, Qu. 9, art. 1.   [2] *Ibid.* Qu. 19, art. 7.

not, as in our case, in that form which, by unwillingness that another should be miserable, involves "a certain sadness rightly called compassion in so far as it makes its own what belongs to another," but in the act of unwillingness that another should suffer, the act which brings relief to the sufferer[1].

This distinction between action and feeling is reminiscent of Augustine's argument that feelings are ascribed to God corresponding to the action which He takes, anger, for example, standing for His punitive judgments. But whereas feeling can properly be attributed to man, since man is, in virtue of his nature, capable of being acted on and changed from without, that cannot be supposed to occur in connexion with God. Moreover, the conception of God's eternal "foreknowledge" introduces a quite new factor. Human feelings have their place under the conditions of the successiveness of human life with its element of surprise and consequent change. But it is just that successiveness, in respect both of His life and of His knowledge, which was excluded from the doctrine of God.

6. PROTESTANT THEOLOGY

Passing to the teaching of the leaders and theologians of the Reformation, we find that as, except in the case of the Socinians and of certain elements among those generally classifiable as Anabaptists, there was no breach with the ancient and the medieval Church in respect of the doctrine of God, the idea of impassibility remains constant. Nothing is said on this point either by

[1] *Summa Theologica*, Qu. 21, art. 3.

Melanchthon in his *Loci Communes* or by Calvin in the *Institutes*. Melanchthon, indeed, shrank from attempts to lay down exact definitions as to the divine nature. At the beginning of the *Loci* he speaks with contempt of those who had tried to penetrate into the "mysteries of the divine" (*divinitatis*), and he has no section dealing with the doctrine of God. But a clue to his attitude may be obtained from the section *De vi legis*, where he speaks of God's revelation of the law working in some the sense of sin and feelings of terror; "because this truly comes to pass it proceeds from God, and Scripture calls this work the judgment, wrath, and fury of God, the aspect or countenance of His anger, and so on." The implication is that human feelings and experiences cannot be directly ascribed to God.

A similar conclusion, clearly expressed, is to be found in Calvin's Commentaries. On Genesis vi, 6 he writes: "the repentance which is here ascribed to God does not properly belong to Him, but has reference to our understanding of Him.... That repentance cannot take place in God easily appears from this single consideration, that nothing happens which is by Him unexpected or unforeseen. The same reasoning and remark applies to what follows, that God was affected with grief. Certainly God is not sorrowful or sad, but remains for ever like Himself in His celestial and happy repose; yet because it could not otherwise be known how great is God's hatred and detestation of sin, therefore the spirit accommodates Himself to our capacity.... This figure which represents God as transferring to Himself what is peculiar to human nature is called ἀνθρωποπάθεια." Again, on Isaiah lxiii, 9, a passage which finds the tenderness of God's love for Israel revealed in His fellowship with them in the experience of their afflictions, he says "in order to move us more powerfully and draw us to Himself, the Lord accommodates himself to the manner of men, by attributing to Himself all the affection, love and (συμπαθεία) compassion which a father can have." And after considering the question of the true reading in the passage and deciding against the insertion of the negative[1], he continues "the Prophet testifies that God, in order to alleviate the distresses and afflictions of His people, Himself bore their burdens; not that He can in any way endure anguish, but by a very customary figure of speech, He assumes and applies to Himself human passions."

The consideration of Luther has been postponed till now because of the way in which his retention of the doctrine of impassibility is crossed by his Christology. Luther was quite definitely not a Monophysite, if the form of his doctrine is in question. But in effect his doctrine amounted to Monophysitism, seeing that his understanding of the meaning of the *communicatio idiomatum* involved the completest reciprocity between the two natures. It will be seen that the distinction which Cyril in his *Epistola Dogmatica* draws between the proper nature of the Word and the body which the Word had made His own vanishes in Luther's exposition. Thus in one of his sermons on St John's Gospel he speaks of Christ's two natures "sharing with one-another their characteristics," and of them as united in one Person in

[1] See R.V. margin. The translations are those published by the Calvin Translation Society.

such wise that what is said of the one nature is also ascribed to the other; for instance, death, while proper to the human nature alone, is also attributed to the Godhead, and we say "God has died." The explanation of this is that "the two natures join their characteristics, and the divine nature gives to the human its characteristics, and, conversely, the manhood gives its to the divine nature[1]." Luther's views come to light in his *Table-Talk*, where he is dealing with the contention that in Christ only the manhood, not the Godhead, suffered, since the Godhead can neither suffer nor die. As against this he affirms that the true faith is that not only the human nature but the divine nature, or the "right true God" has suffered and died for us. Suffering and death are, indeed, experiences which, as they are alien to the divine nature *per se*, cannot be directly attributed to it; but since the divine nature has taken to itself the human, and the two are united in Christ, "it comes about that these two natures in Christ share, the one with the other, their *idiomata* and characteristics. . . . To be born, to suffer, to die, are characteristics of the human nature, of which characteristics the divine nature also becomes sharer in this Person." So Mary is "a right true Mother of God," and as of birth, so of suffering and death: these can be ascribed to the divine nature through the *communicatio idiomatum*. Accordingly one should believe "that everything which essentially belongs to the human nature in Christ is communicated, united and given to the divine nature"; and, conversely, the characteristics of the divine nature are given to the

[1] In the Erlangen edition, vol. xlvii, pp. 175 ff.

human. These statements[1] he follows up with the assertion of the doctrine which has been regarded as the special feature of the Lutheran Christology—that of the ubiquity of Christ's human nature, ascribed in this passage to its non-separability from the divine nature, but also, and more properly, to be conceived of as resulting from "that interpenetration of the divine and the human, to whose complete realization the resurrection and glorification put the finishing stroke[2]."

In sharp contrast with the Lutheran Christology, and in a manner reminiscent of the Arian aversion from the ascription of human experiences and passions to God, we may set Socinus' objection to the Homoousian doctrine, in which is implied an opposition to any theology which brings the divine nature within the region of change and passibility. Socinus argues that to speak of Christ as begotten of the substance of God is repugnant to reason, which does not permit us to think of God as begetting, after the manner of corruptible animals, from His substance, or of the divine essence, which is single in number, as being divided or multiplied[3].

For a more formal treatment of the doctrine of impassibility in Protestant theology we may turn to the *Loci Theologici* of the Lutheran divine, John Gerhard. Starting from the assertion of the changelessness of God, who is pure action without passive potentiality, he argues against Vorstius' assumption of *temporum spatia* in God,

[1] Erlangen edition, vol. LVIII, pp. 34 ff.
[2] Dorner, *Doctrine of the Person of Christ*, Div. II, vol. II, p. 101.
[3] *Christianae Religionis Institutio* (ed. 1656) p. 655.

and the view that in God freedom of will involves changeableness in essence and will. Nor will he allow the Calvinistic distinction between God's absolute decrees in eternity and His saving or condemning men in time according as He sees faith or unbelief[1]. As to the feelings ascribed to God—repentance, happiness, grief, anger, hatred and so on, these "without any disturbance, disorder, opposition from reason or delay in time, and so without any imperfection, are to be understood as ascribed to God $\theta\epsilon o\pi\rho\epsilon\pi\epsilon\hat{\iota}s$, whence comes the canon of the Schoolmen 'Affections In God describe effects'[2]." In a later section he considers the immortality of God, and in reply to the question "whether God is $\dot{a}\pi a\theta\acute{\eta}s$ and impatibilis" says "as God alone is *simpliciter* unchangeable and immortal—so also He alone is absolutely and *simpliciter* impassible. He is infinite being; therefore, on account of this infinity, nothing can act upon Him, since all things except God are finite, and so cannot act on that which is infinite. He is being in its perfect simplicity, and pure action; therefore, because of this simplicity of essence, He cannot be the recipient of the action of another. He is independent being; therefore, because of this independence, nothing can compel or change Him." Accordingly God experiences no real *passio* when blasphemed, such as produces any change, but only a *passio* relative to the intention of the blasphemer[3].

On the Passion of Christ Gerhard avails himself of the Lutheran conception of the *communicatio idiomatum*.

[1] *Loc.* 2, cap. 8, sec. 5 (Berlin, 1864).
[2] *Loc.* 2, cap. 8, sec. 1.   [3] *Loc.* 2, cap. 8, sec. 6.

In the course of a long discussion he says, "to whom truly belongs a subject, to him truly belong the πάθη of that subject." So, "since the Logos has appropriated to Himself human nature and all its characteristics, assuming it into the unity of His person, the passion and death, though according to the natural state not proper to divinity, yet, because of the intimate and ineffable communion of natures and appropriation of the properties of the flesh, do not pertain to the Son of God less than if He had endured them in His divine nature, even as a man is truly and properly said to be wounded, though his body alone is wounded." Further, as there is no "trope" in saying "God is man," just so really do we say "God suffered," and the words are to be accepted in their proper signification; it is not enough to say that the human nature suffered and died[1]. At the same time, Gerhard speaks more carefully than Luther. He will not allow that *passiones* are ascribable to a nature, and refers to "that most certain rule 'Actions and passions belong to a person[2]'"; he rejects such expressions as "Deity suffered[3]."

Among Calvinistic theologians one of the greatest names is that of Turretin. While he does not directly expound the doctrine of impassibility there can be no doubt as to his position. He denies all possibility of change in God, and, after the manner of Calvin, explains that while repentance is attributed to God anthropopathically it is to be understood in a manner worthy of Him, "in respect not of intention, but of event, not

[1] *Loc.* 4, cap. 11, par. 195.
[2] *Loc.* 16, sec. 59.   [3] *Ibid.* par. 198.

of His will but of the thing willed, not of affect and internal grief but of effect and external work, since He
does what a repentant man is accustomed to do." So, in
relation to Genesis vi, 6–8, he interprets the repentance
there spoken of as applying to God's energy which
causes change in what had been made, through its abo-
lition[1]. Among the sixteenth and seventeenth century
confessions of faith express mention of the divine impassibility is made in the Thirty-nine Articles of the
Church of England, and in the Westminster Confession.
But the doctrine, whether mentioned or not, may be
taken as common to all, and its truth is received without
question by such eminent post-Reformation divines as
Pearson, Butler and John Wesley[2].

[1] *Institutio Theologiae elencticae* (Edinburgh, 1847),
Loc. iii, qu. ii.
[2] Passages from them and others are given by Dr Marshall
Randles in his book *The Blessed God. Impassibility.*

CHAPTER II

The Modern Reaction against the Doctrine
of Impassibility

I. THE OCCASIONAL CHARACTER OF
THE REACTION

THE material brought together up to this point shows the existence of a steady and continuous, if not quite unbroken, tradition in Christian theology as to the freedom of the divine nature from all suffering and from any potentiality of suffering. The special problems arising in connexion with Christology do not affect the truth of this conclusion, and, as against Patripassianism, Monophysitism and Theopaschitism, the Church as a whole pursued a course and made distinctions which were intended to be a safeguard against any ascription of passibility to the divine nature, and to rule out any form of doctrine which seemed logically to involve such an error.

Of this tradition the truth is not unchallenged to-day. But whereas it is usually possible to trace stages in the development of a reaction against a particular doctrine or tradition, to show the sources whence the reaction has sprung, and to find help towards agreement or disagreement in the study of some scientific exposition of a contrary or, at least, modified theology, that is by no means the case with the present subject. Reference can be made, as will be seen, to particular writers, and lines of approach to a doctrine of divine passibility can be found in certain currents of modern thought, but it cannot be said that the question has been subjected to methodical theological attention. It is, indeed, interesting to note how completely the issue is ignored in important modern works where one might have expected at least some mention of impassibility as either an important truth of the divine nature or an ill-grounded supposition. Search will be made in vain in *Lux Mundi* or in *Foundations*[1] or in the *Cambridge Theological Essays* or in the Bishop of Oxford's *Manual of Theology* or in Bishop Gore's *Belief in God*. Dr Hall, in his *Dogmatic Theology*, makes no reference to divine impassibility in the volume devoted to the Being and Attributes of God, but has one short statement when he is dealing with the Passion of Christ. The doctrine, he says, means, not "that there is no basis for the biblical ascriptions to God of love and anger, of joy and grieving, and the like," but that "these terms, borrowed as they are from the analogies of finite and temporal experience, are symbolical, and describe affections (*sic*) in God which transcend in mode every temporal process and experience. If God was to suffer *after the human manner*, He had to make human nature His own[2]." Ritschl, in the constructive volume of his *Justification and Reconciliation*[3], makes no contribution,

[1] Except for the implications of a quotation from C. A. Dinsmore's *Atonement in Literature and Life* by Mr W. H. Moberly, on p. 322.

[2] *The Passion and Exaltation of Christ*, pp. 95 f.

[3] Principal Franks in his article in *E.R.E.* draws attention to Ritschl's attachment to Lotze's teaching in respect of his own religious view of God. True though this is, and definitely though Ritschl emphasized divine personality, he says nothing on the subject of passibility.

nor does Kaftan in his *Dogmatik*, though the Ritschlian attitude, especially in the case of Ritschl himself, towards metaphysics in theology renders such silence in the presence of what could be represented as a piece of Greek metaphysics the more surprising. There can be no doubt as to what doctrine Father Pesch the Jesuit theologian would have affirmed as true, but in his *Compendium Theologiae Dogmaticae* he does, in fact, say nothing on the subject. He has a proposition "God is spiritual substance, infinitely perfect," and another "God is immutable and eternal." Certainly it could be argued that either proposition involves impassibility, but it might seem as though some argument or, at least, affirmation would have been in place. In so far as controversy has arisen in recent years it has been concerned with a subject on which dogmatic theologians have kept an extensive silence. Nor have the historians of dogma, like Harnack and Loofs, shown any interest in the matter, though it would have been quite relevant to do so had they felt its importance.

It follows from this that reactions against the idea of impassibility have not taken place in the presence of a strong insistence upon the idea, and that discussions as to the relationship of God to the world have rarely involved any sense of the necessity for an explicit treatment of this subject. Much attention has been devoted to the question of the divine will and purpose for the world, and from this it has been impossible to exclude some consideration of the problem of time and eternity in its relation to the divine life. But as to what consequences, if any, follow in respect of feeling and

M   9 emotion, or how the anthropomorphic language in which the character of the divine life has been pictured should be interpreted, there has been little formal discussion, and nothing like a continuous and connected inquiry.

2 (A). INFLUENCES FROM THE SIDE OF METAPHYSICS

Yet two currents of thought bear upon the subject. The first springs from the side of metaphysics. Principal Franks observes "that philosophy itself has in modern times shown an important movement towards a doctrine of God which admits an element of passibility in His being[1]." He refers, in particular, to Lotze's teaching on divine personality, and quotes a passage from the *Microcosmus*, in which Lotze expresses dissatisfaction with speculation "when it offers to us some self-cognizant Principle of Identity, or some self-conscious Idea of Good, as completely expressing personality." The reason is that "either of these is obviously lacking in an essential condition of all true reality in the capacity of *suffering*[2]." At the same time, Lotze warns against "the transference of the conditions of finite personality to the personality of the Infinite," and especially against any idea that God needs, as we do, the help of stimuli from the external world. What is necessarily true in the case of the finite being, even though for it "the forms of its activity flow from its own inner nature[3]," is not true at all of the Infinite, since "that which is only proxi-

---

[1] *E.R.E.* vol. IX, p. 659.   [2] *Microcosmus*, II, p. 682.
[3] *Ibid.* p. 683.

mately possible for the finite mind, the conditioning of its life by itself, takes place without limit in God, and no contrast of an external world is necessary for Him[1]." As to "what it is that in God corresponds to the primary impulse which the train of ideas in a finite mind receives from the external world," Lotze answers that in any theory of the universe actual movement must be recognized "as an originally given reality," and in a second passage quoted by Principal Franks affirms that "when we characterize the inner life of the Personal God, the current of His thoughts, His feelings, and His will, as everlasting and without beginning, as having never known rest, and having never been roused to movement from some state of quiescence, we call upon imagination to perform a task no other and no greater than that which is required from it by every materialistic or pantheistic view[2]." Further, whereas finite beings have to work under conditions of powers and laws which come to them from without, and the imperfection of their personality is shown in the kind of question which they ask—"What are we ourselves? What is our soul?"—personality "can be perfect only in the Infinite Being which, in surveying all its conditions or actions, never finds any content of that which it suffers or any law of its working, the meaning and origin of which are not transparently plain to it, and capable of being explained by reference to its own nature[3]." What suffering means to God Lotze has not tried to expound; his argument does not pass beyond the assertion of God's

[1] *Microcosmus*, ii, p. 684.   [2] *Ibid*. pp. 684 f.
[3] *Ibid*. p. 686.

capacity for suffering, and of His real independence—in this as in other respects—of the world.

Of relevance also are those philosophical tendencies in modern times which, partly by way of reaction from Hegelianism and from what William James called "monistic absolutism[1]," have led to conceptions of an element of limitation and finitude in God. When philosophical thought reaches the idea of divine personality it comes into relations with the Christian tradition in a manner to which there can be no parallel in world-views which present as the highest stage in their own development and as the final principle of interpretation, the idea of impersonal spirit. On the other hand, insistence on the metaphysical attributes of God, on aseity, simplicity, immutability and so forth, makes it natural for the dogmatic theologian to refuse to draw any real distinction between God and the Absolute, or to think of God as in some sense finite in contrast with the infinity of the Absolute. If, as James says, philosophy and mysticism identify the "*something* larger than ourselves" of religious experience with "a unique God who is the all-inclusive soul of the world[2]," dogmatic theology has not been less forward in emphasizing the unity and infinity of God. A philosophical system which involved a doctrine of God as the greatest of all facts within the Absolute would be regarded by at least the great majority of Christian theologians as widely divergent from Christian theology, and as involving dangers, not indeed comparable to those of polytheism and yet not of a

[1] *The Varieties of Religious Experience*, p. 454.
[2] *Ibid.* p. 525.

wholly different kind[1]. The question with which James ends his final chapter in *The Varieties of Religious Experience* is one which would suggest a doctrine of God all too anthropomorphic in character[2]; and yet, the outlook upon the problem of God and the world to which that question witnesses has not been without its importance and influence in theological statements. Further expression to his conception of God and to his refusal to identify God with the Absolute is given in his Hibbert Lectures entitled *A Pluralistic Universe*. There, on the one hand, he bows the Absolute out altogether, for his statement that he holds that God's "rival and competitor—I feel almost tempted to say his enemy—the absolute, is not only not forced on us by logic, but that it is an improbable hypothesis[3]," is an instance of the figure of speech called meiosis; on the other, he states his belief that "the only God worthy of the name *must* be finite[4]," and, in his final lecture, draws from his argument the conclusion that "the line of least resistance, as it seems to me, both in theology and in philosophy, is to accept, along with the superhuman consciousness, the notion that it is not all-embracing, the notion, in other words, that there is a God, but that he is finite, either in power or in knowledge, or in both at once[5]."

[1] Religious experience cannot, as James points out (p. 525), disprove "the notion of many finite gods." But this is a point where in the interests of religious experience a metaphysical idea—of the one God—may be all-important.

[2] "Who knows whether the faithfulness of individuals here below to their own poor over-beliefs may not actually help God in turn to be more effectively faithful to his own greater tasks?" (*Varieties*, p. 519).   [3] *Pluralistic Universe*, p. 111.
[4] *Ibid.* p. 125.   [5] *Ibid.* p. 311.

From such assertions a very short step leads to the predication of God's passibility; one may, indeed, say that it is inconceivable that the God of Professor James' philosophy should not be passible.

Professor William James regarded Pluralism as a final truth. He had no interest in Monism or Absolutism, and no wish to pass, and no believer in the possibility of passing, from the Many to the One. That was not the case with Professor James Ward. His second series of Gifford Lectures, *The Realm of Ends*, shows that for him pluralism was a principle of the greatest value in epistemology, and that it contained real truth, but was not itself final truth. For James, theism falls within pluralism; for Ward theism is transcendent of pluralism. Two quotations will reveal the wide difference between the two thinkers: retaining the idea of the creation of the world by God, though that idea, like the idea of God, is "altogether transcendent[1]," Ward writes, "no theist can pretend that the world is co-ordinate with God: the divine transcendence is essential to the whole theistic position[2]"; while, summing up his conclusions in his final lecture, he says "we approach theism then as promising to complete pluralism, not as threatening to abolish it, as providing theoretically more unity in the ground of the world, and practically a higher and fuller unity in its meaning and end[3]." Yet while Professor Ward means by "God" something very different from what Professor James means, he agrees with the latter in not equating God with the Absolute, and in recognizing the

[1] *The Realm of Ends*, p. 245.   [2] *Ibid.* p. 243.
[3] *Ibid.* p. 437.

presence in God of an element of limitation and finitude. The Absolute is not simply God, but God-and-the-world. While for the theist, creation does not involve any external limitation of God, yet, if it "is to have any meaning at all it implies internal limitation. . . . God indeed has not been limited from without but he has limited himself[1]." The expression "finite God" Ward characterizes as an "unfortunate term," but accepts what is meant by those who have adopted it, for whom it means "all that God *can* mean, if God implies the world and is not God without it: it means a living God with a living world, not a potter God with a world of illusory clay, not an inconceivable abstraction that is only infinite and absolute, because it is beyond everything and means nothing[2]." Ward's solution, with which his lectures close, of the problem presented by the One and the Many, whereby a unification of extreme views on either side may be reached, is through the idea of Love. The one great mystery which Christianity affirms, that of the Incarnation, has a further cosmic relevance. In the love of God is the explanation of the world's creation to be found. "The world is God's self-limitation, self-renunciation, might we venture to say[3]?"

Professor Ward never enters upon the question of passibility or impassibility, which is, perhaps, curious in view both of the general character of his argument and

[1] *Realm of Ends*, p. 243.
[2] *Ibid*. p. 444. Prof. Ward says that the term "finite God" was devised by those who, in contrast with what they regarded as its implication of "imperfection and dependence," upheld a sheerly absolutist doctrine of God.
[3] *Ibid*. p. 453.

of the attention he devotes to the problem of evil. He comes very near to it in his supplementary note on "The Temporal and the Eternal," where he discusses the meaning of the divine perfection with special reference to unchangeableness. But in this note, as in the next on "The Divine Experience," it is with the nature of God's knowledge that he is specially concerned. "God's life," he says, "is always perfect. So far unchangeableness may be attributed to God, as it can be to none beside." That such a life does not exclude movement he maintains: "unless all activity is essentially an imperfection, there is no contradiction in Aristotle's doctrine of pure or perfect activity (ἐνέργεια ἀκινησίας)." But as to whether the affirmation of passibility would be incompatible with the divine perfection, he says nothing.

In the Gifford Lectures of another eminent philosopher we find a deliberate conclusion reached at this point. Professor Pringle-Pattison in his work *The Idea of God in the Light of Recent Philosophy*, after declaring in his closing pages that "to reach any credible theory of the relation of God and man we must...profoundly transform the traditional idea of God," and commenting on attempts made to reconcile the world as we know it with the notion of God's Creatorship, goes on to express his dissent from a doctrine of God not unfairly describable "as a fusion of the primitive monarchical ideal with Aristotle's conception of the Eternal Thinker." What is common to both conceptions is "the idea of a self-centred life and a consequent aloofness from the world." He quotes a remark of Erdmann's in his *Grundriss der Geschichte der Philosophie* that "the time had not yet come when God would be known as the God that took on Himself πόνος, labour, without which the life of God would be one of heartless ease, troubled with no thing, while with it alone He is Love and Creator.' From the truth of sacrifice, of losing one's life to find it, as supplying "the deepest insight into human life," Professor Pringle-Pattison argues, in a manner which recalls Professor Ward's closing sentences, that here also is "the open secret of the universe." "That," he says, "is the conclusion to which we have been led up more than once already in the course of these lectures: no God, or Absolute, existing in solitary bliss or perfection, but a God who lives in the perpetual giving of himself, who shares the life of his finite creatures, bearing in and with them the whole burden of their finitude, their sinful wanderings and sorrows, and the suffering without which they cannot be made perfect[1]." Accordingly "for a metaphysic which has emancipated itself from physical categories, the ultimate conception of God is not that of a pre-existent Creator but, as it is for religion, that of the eternal Redeemer of the world. This perpetual process is the very life of God, in which, besides the effort and the pain, He tastes, we must believe, the joy of victory won[2]." The God thus described is much more than the *primus inter pares* of William James' pluralistic philosophy, but His impassibility is given up as untrue alike for religion and for philosophy.

[1] *Idea of God*, p. 411.
[2] *Ibid.* p. 412; cf. the whole section, pp. 399–417.

2 (B). INFLUENCES FROM THE SIDE OF
NATURAL SCIENCE

The second current of thought comes in, though indirectly, from the side of natural science. It is not the concern of the scientist to say what is the ultimate explanation and character of those forces in nature of whose presence he is cognizant. But what his investigations reveal will be of value to the theologian who finds in the revelation signs of the character of God's working. In particular, the theologian sees in scientific reactions against mechanistic interpretations of natural processes, and in favour of a greater emphasis upon the free movements of the immanent vital forces, a development which harmonizes with his own belief that the living God is not far away from nature, His creation, any more than He is from men, His children. The life to whose energy and fruitfulness the scientist bears witness is for the theologian a life in which God is present. The long vistas of the evolutionary process suggest for him a deep wonder for the slow, but patient and purposeful, operations of God. So far from a recognition of evolution meaning the repudiation of teleology, the theologian of to-day finds in the revelations of science the illumination of a profounder teleology than any which was possible for Paley. Even though he should feel that more needed to be said, and that that extra element included something different, he would not dissent from the general implications of the statement that "there is one grand progressive movement from the beginning to the farthest limits of our imaginations,—

one theme and one all-sufficient God, who, in a world of conflict and through conflict, has carried His creation from one stage of achievement to another[1]."

Certainly it is a world of conflict. And though the theist, at least he who accepts, as Professor Ward holds that the theist—we may say the real theist—must accept, as true the transcendence of God, will believe that God is above the conflict, he will also believe that in some real way God is in it. And it is not difficult to see how from this may arise a further belief that in this conflict God Himself suffers. So we find a writer in a book whose purpose is to show the bearing of the doctrine of evolution upon theology saying that "We, and all organisms, are subordinate, yet intrinsic parts of Him our whole, and, if one member of His Body suffers, He suffers in sympathy with it. Every sorrow or sin carries with it friction, sickness, a lack of harmony in the whole. Not only is it literally true that 'the whole creation groaneth until now,' but God Himself feels the pain of our suffering and sin. If God 'creates evil' He shares its stab with us. '*I know your sorrows*' [2]." Both in philosophy, and in connexion with the suggestions of natural science, we can discover tendencies which find a response, from the theological side, in an abandonment of a rigid doctrine of divine impassibility. But it is not at present a matter of more than individual response. There has been nothing like any general theological readjustment. Nor, in every case, is an influence upon theology of philosophy or science to be observed.

[1] F. H. Johnson, *God in Evolution*, p. 51.
[2] J. R. Cohu, *Through Evolution to the Living God*, p. 185.

3. THE REACTION ILLUSTRATED IN THEO-LOGICAL WORKS OF THE LAST SIXTY YEARS

Reference may be made first to a brief but interesting discussion of the meaning of God's "Blessedness" by the Danish Bishop Martensen in his *Dogmatics*, which was translated into English in 1866. Blessedness he describes as "the eternal *peace* of love, which is higher than all reason; it is the sabbath of love in its state of eternal perfection." But "love's eternal rest is eternal *activity*," and this difficulty arises, that while "God must be conceived of as self-sufficient and needing no one," yet "His blessedness must be conceived of as conditional upon the perfecting of His Kingdom; because divine love can satisfy itself only as it is bliss-giving, only therefore as it becomes all in all." "The only way," he continues, "to solve this contradiction, is to assume that God has a twofold life—a life in Himself of unclouded peace and self-satisfaction, and a life in and with His creation, in which He not only submits to the conditions of finitude, but even allows His power to be limited by the sinful will of man." It is to this latter that we must refer those Biblical ideas of divine grief and other feelings "which plainly imply a limitation of the divine blessedness." But this limitation "is again swallowed up in the inner life of perfection which God lives in total independence of His creation, and in triumphant prospect of the fulfilment of His great designs. We may therefore say with the old theosophic writers, 'in the Outer Chambers is sadness, but in the inner ones unmixed joy'[1]."

---

[1] *Dogmatics*, sec. 51, p. 101.

Very similar, though without the same sharp differentiation between the two states of the divine life, are the conclusions arrived at by Dr A. J. Mason in his Manual of Christian Doctrine, *The Faith of the Gospel.* God is impassible "in the same sense as He might be called exempt from actions." He is "unvaryingly the same," and "does not go through a series of transient phases, like us." At the same time, "we are compelled to think of God as engaged in a course of action in His relation to the world, and we are compelled to think of Him as reacted upon by it in turn, and, as He follows its development, experiencing now satisfaction and now pain. Impassibility is not the same as unfeeling. If words mean anything, God is capable of grief and joy, of anger and of gratification; though there is nothing which can force such states of feeling upon Him without His being willing to undergo them." God is, indeed, "eternally happy"; He has in Himself "every element of perfect bliss." But in that bliss is included the capacity for suffering; "love unable to manifest itself through a true self-sacrifice, would be love unsatisfied." So in the Biblical phrases concerning God's feeling we have "not mere metaphors, but substantial truths. Only we must remember that no storms of grief can shake the permanent serenity of God in its inmost depths, inasmuch as God sees the end from the beginning and knows Himself to be able to overcome at last all that now causes sorrow to Him and to those whom He loves[1]."

Another widely read work on doctrinal theology is Dr W. N. Clarke's *An Outline of Christian Theology.*

[1] *Faith of the Gospel*, pp. 32 f. in the 3rd edition, revised, of 1890.

Like Martensen and Dr Mason he asserts "the perfect blessedness of God." But he finds nothing incompatible with this in the belief that God is put to real suffering and has to carry a real burden because of Man's sin; "we need to remember, or to learn, the great truth that the endurance of redemptive suffering is the highest bliss. To a holy being there is no worthier or more welcome joy than the endurance of whatever may be necessary for the deliverance of souls from sin. God alone knows to the full that noble gladness, and He knows it perpetually; but even we can see that it is a real joy[1]." And so, for the interpretation of Christ's sufferings, these should be regarded as having been "the true representative symbol and proclamation of what goes on perpetually in God. From them God wished the world to learn that sin is put away only through the redemptive suffering of holy love, which He Himself is gladly bearing, and which Christ, His representative and expression, endured before the eyes of men[2]."

That the passion of Christ reveals on the plane of human history a truth which belongs to the capacities of the divine nature, and was in actual operation even before the Incarnation, is proclaimed in a number of modern works on the Atonement. Horace Bushnell's treatise *The Vicarious Sacrifice* was published in 1866, and was one of the first treatments of the Atonement to break away from the rigid standards of Protestant orthodoxy. The second chapter is entitled "The Eternal Father in Vicarious Sacrifice." Starting from the truth

[1] *Christian Theology*, p. 343, in the 19th edition, of 1912.
[2] *Ibid.* p. 346.

that "love is a principle of vicarious sacrifice," Bushnell
argues that this is true of God before the coming of
Christ. As the most real burdens of Jesus were those
that came upon His mind, so "in these burdens God, as
the Eternal Father, suffered before Him[1]." Bushnell
points to many texts in the Old Testament which express "the painful sympathy and deep burden" of God's
feeling. "It is," he says, "as if there were a cross unseen, standing on its undiscovered hill, far back in the
ages, out of which were sounding always, just the same
deep voice of suffering love and patience, that was heard
by mortal ears from the sacred hill of Calvary[2]." Whatever we may affirm of Christ's vicarious sacrifice, "we
are to affirm in the same manner of God. The whole
Deity is in it, in it from eternity, and will to eternity be.
We are not to conceive that our Blessed Saviour is some
other and better side of Deity, a God composing and
satisfying God; but that all there is in Him expresses
God, even as He is, and has been of old—such a Being
in His love that He must needs take our evils on His
feeling, and bear the burden of our sin[3]."

Principal Simon, in the earlier of his two soteriological works, *The Redemption of Man*, comes into
touch with the question, in the first place in connexion
with "The Anger of God," the truth of which he is
concerned to vindicate. He outlines different views
which have been held, and expresses his own agreement
with those who, like Tertullian and Lactantius whom
he quotes, have maintained that "anger in God is the

[1] *Vicarious Sacrifice*, p. 23.   [2] *Ibid.* p. 31.
[3] *Ibid.* p. 35.

archetype of anger in man, that the two are in essence one[1]." He considers objections which may be raised, among others "that to ascribe anger to God is to interfere with His absoluteness; on the one hand, because it involves His being subject to the influence of the creature; on the other, because an emotion like anger, if not indeed emotion as such, is impossible to the Absolute." He answers that it is of God's own will as expressed in creation, if the conduct of His creatures affects Him, and that if emotion is unworthy of God then we must surrender such an idea as that of His joy over a prodigal's return: "if God must be essentially impassible, unless He is to cease being God, then all our talk of His Fatherly sympathy with us and joy at our faithfulness and the like has no real meaning[2]." Later on, in his chapter entitled "Passio Christi," he speaks of the intensification of the sufferings of the Logos, in whom humanity subsists, in the period before the Incarnation[3], of the *limitation* involved in the Incarnation as "a form of suffering[4]," and of the relation to sin in which Christ stood as being the Logos, "the mediator of the divine immanence in creation, especially in man[5]." For since, "speaking after the manner of men, we may say that human corruption sent up into the conscious life of Deity certain disturbing elements through that sub-conscious side by which He was in immediate, generative, creative, sustentative, *i.e.* immanent contact with the intelligent creature[6]," an intenser influence

---

[1] *The Redemption of Man*, 1889, p. 220.
[2] *Ibid.* pp. 254 f.   [3] *Ibid.* p. 299.   [4] *Ibid.* p. 306.
[5] *Ibid.* p. 321.   [6] *Ibid.* p. 322.

upon His inner sub-conscious nature of the darkness of evil must have occurred during the Incarnate life.

Dr Simon returns to the subject of God's emotions in his later work *Reconciliation by Incarnation*[1]. One of the results of sin is, he affirms, a disturbance in the divine feelings. But, in a manner which recalls Martensen, and to which there is no parallel in *The Redemption of Man*, he goes on to draw distinctions as to the nature and scope of this disturbance. God, in His own essence, "cannot be injured by anything that the creature may do." On the other hand, because of the distinction which may be drawn between the divine nature and its expressions, while "He in Himself abides unaltered," yet "as to His emotions or feelings, these cannot but be affected by the conduct and state of the creatures that He has brought into existence and sustains." But this does not mean that the creature has any power of affecting God contrary to God's own determination, since "in laying Himself open to human action God is carrying out His own purpose[2]." The Biblical phraseology as to the divine feelings testifies to a real truth.

The light which the death of Christ throws upon God's sorrow over human sin is emphasized by Dr Vincent Tymms in his Angus Lecture on *The Christian Idea of Atonement*[3]. He calls attention to the inevitable inadequacy of human thought and language, to the fact that "all our terms are analogical, and that the self-consciousness of God must needs be unsearchable and unutterable." Nevertheless, the truth of human like-

[1] 1898.   [2] *Reconciliation by Incarnation*, pp. 147 f.
[3] 1904.

ness to God and the truth of the Incarnation point away from a doctrine of impassibility. If we draw back from the admission that God can be grieved, then neither shall we be able to speak of His pity or love; "we shall be committed to a denial of all relations, and then the only God left to us will be the infinite iceberg of metaphysics." Again, "if we are forbidden to find in Christ's sorrow a sacramental sign of something in God which is thus expressed to human minds, then we must discard the idea that Christ reveals the Love of God, or His Righteousness, His Holiness, His hatred of sin[1]." In words of Christ, especially in the Parable of the Prodigal Son, Dr Tymms finds a revelation of God's sorrowing love, while to the preciousness of the Cross belongs its power to show "that God is not a mere passionless watcher of an agonizing evolution, but is Himself a partaker of the universal travail, and has been constrained by love to take the chief labour on Himself[2]."

One of the strongest repudiations of the doctrine of impassibility is contained in Dr Fairbairn's work, *The Place of Christ in Modern Theology*[3]. "Sin was," he says, "as it were, the sorrow in the heart of His happiness. Theology has no falser idea than that of the impassibility of God. If He is capable of sorrow, He is capable of suffering; and were He without the capacity for either, He would be without any feeling of the evil of sin or the misery of man. But to be passible is to be capable of sacrifice; and in the presence of sin the capability could not but become the reality. The being of

[1] *Christian Idea of Atonement*, pp. 311–13.
[2] *Ibid.* p. 325.   [3] 1893.

evil in the universe was to God's moral nature an offence and a pain, and through His pity the misery of man became His sorrow." In the light of this belief he interprets the Cross. It was not the Son alone who suffered, but the surrender of Him to that experience "as it was the act, represented the sacrifice and the passion, of the whole Godhead[1]."

Dr G. B. Stevens takes up the same position in his soteriological treatise, *The Christian Doctrine of Salvation*[2]. A love which cannot bear the burdens of the sin and misery of others is unintelligible to us. But the divine love is not of such a kind; "it *is* a love kindred to our own—only immeasurably profounder—which we see illustrated in the holy mystery of Christ's cross and passion;...if Christ gave his life in utmost sacrifice for man, it is because there is in the being of God himself the possibility of vicarious suffering which, so far from marring his blessedness, is one of the elements of that matchless perfection whose name is love[3]." So, for Dr Stevens, there is a threefold cord binding together the Christian life and the sacrifice of Christ and the nature of God; and "the cross is the emblem of the Christian character because it symbolizes what is deepest and most characteristic in Christ, and it symbolizes what is deepest in Christ because it expresses what is central in God—the eternal love, the eternal sympathy and self-giving, which, in turn, involve the immeasurable sorrow of God over sin[4]." Great emphasis is laid upon

[1] *The Place of Christ*, p. 484.　　　[2] 1905.
[3] *Christian Doctrine of Salvation*, pp. 445 f.
[4] *Ibid.* p. 481.

the suffering of God in Mr C. A. Dinsmore's book, *Atonement in Literature and Life*[1]. The thought moves from the love and pity of Jesus to the compassion of the Eternal Christ or Word, and so, finally, to the sorrow of God. The Eternal Christ, "the spirit of Jesus in its infinite nature," who is, "so to speak, that part of God which is ever present in the processes of nature and history," since He is "inexplicably associated with mankind...must suffer. The sufferings of God in the eternal forth-putting of Himself which we call Christ is a distinctive doctrine of Christianity." If God is not as the Epicurean divinities, utterly detached from the affairs and sorrows of men, but as compassionate as Jesus, then "such love must be thought of as forever suffering for the evils of the world." For if the nature of Jesus is to be conceived of "as eternal in its essence," then "a belief in the passibility of God is unavoidable." So Calvary is the symbol and expression in time of an eternal truth; "there was a cross in the heart of God before there was one planted on the green hill outside of Jerusalem. And now that the cross of wood has been taken down, the one in the heart of God abides, and it will remain so long as there is one sinful soul for whom to suffer." This, however, is not the whole truth; "the Christian doctrine of God would be inferior to that of the Greeks, did it not supplement this teaching of the infinite passibility of God with the assertion that the Almighty abides in perfect felicity. In him is completeness of joy because he sees the end from the beginning[2]."

[1] 1906.
[2] *Atonement in Literature and Life*, pp. 229–33.

Substantially the same doctrine appears in a writer who represents a rigid form of Protestant orthodoxy far removed from the theology of Dr Stevens, and still further from the general outlook of Mr Dinsmore. But, like them, Dr Campbell Morgan sees the passion of the Cross against the background of the passion in the heart of God. So he teaches that "that which we see in the Cross did not begin at the point of the material Cross.... In the moment in which man sinned against God, God gathered into His own heart of love the issue of that sin, and it is not by the death of a Man, but by the mystery of the passion of God, that He is able to keep His face turned in love towards wandering men, and welcome them as they turn back to Him. Had there been no passion in His heart, no love, no suffering of Deity, no man could have returned to Him....He has gathered up into His own Being, not by mechanical effort, but by the very necessity of His nature, all the suffering which issues from sin." But this man could not understand, unless it were manifested in time; "and therefore God came into human form and human life, to the actuality of human suffering, on the green hill and upon the rugged Cross, working out into visibility all the underlying truth of the passion of His love, that men seeing it, might understand it, and put their trust in Him. Therefore by the actual, historic and material death, the reconciliation of man is alone possible[1]."

Mr S. A. McDowell's work, *Evolution and the Need of Atonement*[2], is a contribution to soteriology from the side of natural science. To man's development the fact

[1] *The Bible and the Cross*, 1909, pp. 49–51.   [2] 1912.

of sin imposes an unsurmountable obstacle, unless the consequences of sin can be removed, and the way opened to the ultimate attainment of perfection. Such liberation, and the resulting progress, were impossible apart from pain. And God was ready to do all that was necessary to restore communion between Himself and man, and thus to bring back to man his freedom; "by Himself entering into the pangs of spirit fettered by matter; the night-mare struggle of the creature, reaching out into the Beyond and always held back; the unceasing grapple with limitations; God becomes one with His creation[1]." There is no limit to God's self-sacrifice, His altruism; "not only does He identify Himself with the pain of the world's becoming, in order to complete the unity of the spiritual world and to assume before mankind the Headship of all the spiritual hierarchy; but He takes upon Himself the awful burden of suffering that sin has brought into the world[2]."

So the way is opened to freedom and salvation; what man must do is to identify himself "with the world-altruism that Jesus came to vindicate[3]." So long as any good remains in a man, "Christ's death can save him." Yet this thought is no "incentive to laxity." Final loss, through the extinction of all goodness in a man, is possible. "Above all we must never forget that each sin we commit in very truth inflicts suffering on God[4]."

In a chapter of deep religious feeling, Dr Douglas White, the author of *Forgiveness and Suffering*[5], reaches

[1] *Evolution and the Need for Atonement*, p. 146.
[2] *Ibid*. p. 148.   [3] *Ibid*. p. 149.
[4] *Ibid*. pp. 152 f.   [5] 1913.

his conviction of the passibility of God from a consideration of the costliness of forgiveness. Where there is real forgiveness, there is also pain for the one who forgives. That is true of man; it is manifested in the life and teaching of Jesus; and what is true of the Son is true of the Father whom He reveals. The objection that God who is omnipotent and unchangeable cannot suffer is met by the answer that God is love. "Now love is passible; and if God is love, God is passible.... If God's love be infinite, then He can suffer infinitely too. The doctrine of the impassibility of God, taken in its widest sense, is the greatest heresy that ever smirched Christianity; it is not only false, it is the antipodes of truth.... That God Almighty does and can suffer in relation to His sinful creatures,—this is a cardinal doctrine of Christianity[1]." Such love, Dr White argues, is "the only omnipotence," nor is it inconsistent with the true meaning of the divine unchangeableness. So, "passibility in God, involving as it does love and suffering, need not be regarded as the contradiction of that power and stability which are necessary attributes of the divine. For love alone assures constancy of purpose, and love alone can carry the citadel of an estranged heart[2]."

The view that God "suffers in relation to sin" Dr White claims that the Christian Church has never, to his knowledge, denied. He himself would accept a doctrine of impassibility which meant God's freedom from passions "which might affect the justice of His actions and His orderly conduct of the universe[3]." He

[1] *Forgiveness and Suffering*, pp. 83 f.
[2] *Ibid.* pp. 85 f.   [3] *Ibid.* p. 88.

would repudiate any idea of God as involuntarily subjected to pain from without. But when God voluntarily
limits Himself, as in creation, then it is of His own
choice that He takes the path of suffering. That there
is joy for God in His sacrificial suffering Dr White believes, but not that in the perfection of His love the pain
is extinguished; "if the perfections of God make His
self-sacrifice a joy, they also intensify His distress at the
touch of unrighteousness. And each of these truths
within the divine being is seen reflected in the historical
crucifixion[1]." It is "in the certain confidence of the
ultimate triumph of forgiving love" that God endures
the pain of the present. Dr White, like Mr Dinsmore,
interprets the meaning of the process for God by reference to God's assurance of the end. So, returning to
the costliness of forgiveness, he sums up his convictions:
"as Jesus had to suffer in order that He might forgive,
so can God's forgiveness proceed only out of a wounded
heart; and as Christ was made perfect through suffering,
so we may truly say that God's love, passing through
suffering to forgiveness, seeks its proper crown, and
works out its own inherent perfection[2]."

Though lacking the particular application to the conditions of forgiveness, the teaching of Canon Storr is
essentially the same as that of Dr White. It is given at
some length in the chapter headed "God suffers with
the World" in *The Problem of the Cross*[3]. God is indeed
transcendent, but He is also "immanent and operative
in the time-process and in the evolution of the universe[4]."

---

[1] *Forgiveness and Suffering*, p. 93.   [2] *Ibid.* p. 94.
[3] 1919.   [4] *The Problem of the Cross*, p. 113.

He does not dwell "in some Olympian calm"; rather, "as Jesus suffered on earth from man's sin, so does God suffer....The Divine Love revealed in and mediated by Jesus, eternally suffers from our sin." To speak of God as impassible means that He is not subject to human infirmities. But if He has the attributes of personality He "must be able to love, sympathize and suffer[1]."

God's suffering results not from limitation from without, but from self-limitation. The truth of God's love and of His immanence gives us the background of the Cross. "Three great thoughts come before us. First, the thought that God is suffering with His world, sharing its sorrows, and entering into the struggles of His creation. Secondly, the thought that the Cross of Christ was no after-thought on the part of God, but was the expression at a definite historical period of something which represents an eternal actuality in the divine life.... The third thought is the same thought, but rather differently focussed in the doctrine of the Holy Spirit, the thought of God perpetually working in men's lives, summoning them to service and the cross, uniting Himself with men that He may give to men His own life of self-sacrifice[2]." Canon Storr carefully distinguishes this doctrine from that of a finite God, who may be in danger of defeat. In the true Christian doctrine, "God suffers because He chooses to suffer. His love freely creates its own burden, freely chooses to carry its cross. There is nothing derogatory to God's majesty here[3]." And Canon Storr comes very near to Martensen's distinction

[1] *The Problem of the Cross*, p. 114.
[2] *Ibid.* p. 124.　　　　　　[3] *Ibid.* p. 125.

between the spheres of the divine life. Can we not, he asks, hold that God suffers with the world, "and at the same time hold that He is a centre of peace? Strife and struggle belong to time, not to eternity. God dwells in eternity.... If He enters into our limitations, He is at the same time beyond them. Hence, while His love really suffers from human sin and feels all earth's pains, it remains a victorious love, which knows no defeat, and is at each moment triumphant[1]." More recently, Canon Storr has expressed the same doctrine in his chapter "God and Man" in *The Inner Life*[2]. In the evolutionary process God suffers with His creation; "He enters into it, experiences the struggle, feels the pain of the whole of His creation. He does so because it is love's nature to go out of itself in self-sacrifice. Our own sufferings may not be fully explained by this thought of God, but a new light is thrown upon them when they are thus linked to God's sufferings[3]."

One of the most remarkable books in which the idea of the passibility of God has been set forth is *The World's Redemption*[4] by the late Mr C. E. Rolt. It presents a comprehensive philosophy of the world's life in relation to God, and its positive and challenging character raises in the clearest form issues of a fundamental character. The underlying conviction which controls the whole development of the writer's thought is that the only omnipotence which God possesses is that of love. God's one power in the face of evil is the power of patient love, and in this love, through suffering, lies the only way to

---

[1] *The Problem of the Cross*, p. 126.   [2] 1924 or 1925.
[3] *The Inner Life*, p. 17.   [4] 1913.

the conquest of evil. In God "all suffering has been glorified into rapture, and the evil which He suffers is the condition of His perfect bliss and triumph. This is the mystery of the Cross, a mystery which lies at the centre of God's eternal Being[1]." The world was never, from the first, a perfect world, it always contained evil; this evil, in every form, is utterly hateful to God, and is endured by Him in silent patience. "The whole earth groans aloud in anguish and degradation. And inwards, at the very centre of the world, these cries strike upon the ear of God, who hears them with an infinite grief; for, at the inmost core of all things, there is no mere creative mind or vital force: there is a Human Heart, and that Heart is broken[2]." The special vileness of sin consists in the fact that it is wrong done to One, "Who, by the very nature of His omnipotence, is bound and tied hand and foot in the midst of this evil world, and is obliged to bear, not only the physical sufferings of the whole creation, but also the far more bitter pain of human malice and sin[3]." But there is not mere suffering; because suffering is for God the way to victory, in suffering and the patient endurance of it God has joy and peace. The very fact that God is God is revealed in His suffering. "Man," says Mr Rolt, "is a noble and a god-like being only so far as he, in patient love, has suffered; and therefore God is God only in the fact that He, in perfect patience, has undergone all that the word suffering can possibly mean," a declaration from which certain

---

[1] *The World's Redemption*, p. 127.
[2] *Ibid.* p. 183.
[3] *Ibid.* p. 185.

conclusions are drawn as to the character of the suffering of Christ[1]. How thoroughly Mr Rolt works out his central idea of love and love's suffering in connexion with the life of God, one further quotation will show: "God is a Trinity because He is perfect love; and therefore the Holy Trinity is one perfect and ineffable bliss. And that bliss consists, not so much in the absence of pain, but rather in the victory over all its pangs. In the eternal joy of the Trinity all pain is, not avoided, but overcome and transmuted into glory; for only thus can joy be perfect and therefore truly itself.—But eternity is not independent of time: it is time's crown and goal. God must, therefore, pass through time to attain to His own eternal Being. And in this passage He must experience the pain as untransmuted pain. Only thus can He transmute it, and, by it, attain to His own perfection[2]."

Mr Rolt's book is commended, and its theme to some extent expounded in an article by Canon Streeter on "The Suffering of God" in the *Hibbert Journal* for April 1914. The first part of the article gives Canon Streeter's own view, and was written before Mr Rolt's book had appeared and come to his notice. After noticing Greek and Hebrew ideas of the transcendence and absoluteness of God, and arguing that, so far as the imagination is concerned, it is the Arian view of the remote, aloof God, rather than the Athanasian conception of God as truly revealed in Christ, which has prevailed in Christian theology, he claims that "capacity

---

[1] *The World's Redemption*, p. 228.
[2] *Ibid.* p. 247.

to feel, and if need be to suffer, is surely involved in the very conception of God as love[1]." And, for the reconciliation of faith in the goodness of God with the fact of the world's evil, he urges, "boldly press home the principles of St John and Athanasius, 'He that hath seen me hath seen the Father,' the Father is essentially as the Son, and all is changed. God Himself is seen to share the suffering He allows. More than that: by an eternal activity of which the Death of Christ is both a symbol and also an essential part, He is everlastingly, at the cost of His own effort and His own pain, redeeming and perfecting the world He made[2]." To one point in this statement I would draw attention in view of the divergence there between Canon Streeter and Mr Rolt. Canon Streeter speaks of God as allowing suffering. Mr Rolt denies that God ever allows evil; on the contrary, it is just because God does not allow evil that evil exists; if God allowed it, it would cease to be.

The War gave a great impetus to the discussion of the relation of God to the evil of the world. The view expressed in the words "the person whom I am really sorry for is God" represented an opinion with which probably a considerable number of those who awoke to the consciousness of the need for a theology and a theodicy would have agreed. And a theology which found its central emphasis in belief in a suffering God, expressed in a popular and unconventional manner, became widely known through the writings and poems of Mr Studdert-Kennedy, especially through his earliest

[1] *Hibbert Journal*, vol. XII, p. 605.
[2] *Ibid.* p. 606.

book, *The Hardest Part*[1]. His thought is as clear-cut as Mr Rolt's, his affirmations and denials as decided. "One needs," he says, "a Father, and a Father must suffer in His children's suffering. I could not worship the passionless potentate... I don't know or love the Almighty potentate, my only real God is the suffering Father revealed in the sorrow of Christ[2]." This belief is developed throughout the book. As Creator, God was no omnipotent monarch, but He "was forced to limit Himself... He had to bind Himself with chains and pierce Himself with nails, and take upon Himself the travail pangs of creation. The universe was made as it is because it is the only way it could be made, and this way lays upon God the burden of many failures and of eternal strain—the sorrow of God the Father which Christ revealed[3]." The same holds good of human history: "God, the Father God of Love, is everywhere in history, but nowhere is He Almighty. Ever and always we see Him suffering, striving, crucified, but conquering"; "if the Christian religion means anything, it means that God is Suffering Love, and that all real progress is caused by the working of Suffering Love in the world[4]." Once more, political progress and political hopes, the profound truth present in the democratic idea, are incompatible with the doctrine of God's passionless

[1] 1918. I do not draw upon Mr Wells' conceptions of God as outlined towards the end of *Mr Britling sees it through*, and fully disclosed in *God the Invisible King*, since, whatever be thought of Mr Wells' doctrine, it does not fall within the scope of a survey limited to *Christian* theology.

[2] *The Hardest Part*, p. 10.

[3] *Ibid.* p. 26.   [4] *Ibid.* pp. 41–4.

omnipotence: "in their hearts all true men worship one God—the naked, wounded, bloody, but unconquered and unconquerable Christ. This is the God for whom the heart of democracy is longing, and after whom it is blindly, blunderingly, but earnestly groping[1]." And as the War sounded the doom of absolute monarchy upon earth, so we must abandon the idea of such power as vested in God: "we can no longer interpret ultimate reality in the terms of absolute monarchy if we are to reach the hearts of men[2]." The great truths of the spiritual life are correspondingly re-interpreted. Prayer is, essentially, not "an act of passive submission[3]," not a request to be spared suffering, but "the means of communication by which the suffering and triumphant God meets His band of volunteers and pours His Spirit into them, and sends them out to fight, to suffer, and to conquer in the end[4]." Of the Holy Communion he writes, "coming to the Sacrament is coming to the Cross, and coming to the Cross is coming to God, the only God, Whose body is forever broken and Whose blood is ever shed, until the task of creative redemption shall at last be all complete[5]." Again, the history of the Church and what men see in the Church is incompatible with "the vision of the regnant God upon a throne, calm, serene, and passionless, ruling the world with a wave of the hand[6]." The real truth about the Church is that it is "the broken, battered, bleeding, but deathless body of the suffering God revealed in Christ[7]."

[1] *The Hardest Part*, p. 95.   [2] *Ibid.* p. 99.
[3] *Ibid.* p. 111.   [4] *Ibid.* p. 117.
[5] *Ibid.* p. 131.   [6] *Ibid.* p. 149.   [7] *Ibid.* p. 148.

The thoughts of *The Hardest Part* came to its author on the battlefields of the West, and their intensity, both in idea and in expression, reveals clearly enough the pressure and tension of such tremendous experiences. But the same theology reappears, and as something which belongs to the heart of religious truth, in later works, such as *Lies!*[1], *Food for the Fed-up*[2], and *The Wicket Gate*[3]. Over it, as over Mr Rolt's world-view, might be written as a text the words δεῖ τὸν Θεὸν παθεῖν.

We have already met with Canon Streeter's doctrine. It remains the same in his contribution to the volume *God and the Struggle for Existence*[4]. With him were associated the Archbishop of Dublin and Miss Dougall. Dr D'Arcy, writing on "Love and Omnipotence," approves that idea of a God who strives and suffers, which had become "the inspiration of a fresh and popular creed[5]." Its value is real, for "if we have reason to believe that God shares in every human grief, that no lonely sufferer endures his agony apart from the sympathy and fellowship of God, that every sacrifice made is a sacrifice on God's part as well as on man's, and that, in suffering, God is calling on us to join Him in His age-long struggle against evil, we have a view of the world and of human life which gives to all genuine moral

[1] 1919, pp. 132–55.
[2] 1921, pp. 49–71, 171–204, especially 202–4 and the association of redemption with creation. "Calvary is the revelation in human terms of what Creation—Creation in that larger, truer sense which includes Redemption—means to God."
[3] 1923, pp. 47–51.   [4] 1919.
[5] *God and the Struggle for Existence*, p. 17.

effort, whether pleasurable or painful, an intrinsic worth which cannot be estimated[1]." That this is a reasonable belief seems to the Archbishop to be implied in God's nature as love, from which we may conclude that God shares in our joys and our sorrows.

Miss Dougall, in her chapter on "Power—Human and Divine," in which her ideas as to the real nature of power present much affinity with those of Mr Rolt and Mr Studdert-Kennedy, also refers to the divine passibility. "If," she says, "we mean anything by the 'fatherhood of God,' we mean that in sympathy God must have been with them in this world-system of cause and effect, and that through all the school of experience He must by sympathy have rejoiced in their joys and suffered in their pains[2]." It is to be noted that while this is a doctrine of a suffering God, there is not the same stress laid upon God's own sufferings as in the writers just mentioned. God is rather regarded as sharing in the sufferings of others by sympathy than as enduring His own. His passion is compassion.

Canon Streeter writes on "The Defeat of Pain." In his emphasis he goes beyond Miss Dougall, but there seems to be more allowance for another side of the truth about God than appears in Mr Studdert-Kennedy's work. This is how he expresses his belief: "God does not stand outside the world serenely contemplating the misery and the strife. He is no doubt in a sense outside and beyond the world, but He is also inside it—immanent in it, as the philosophers say; and by the fact of

[1] *God and the Struggle for Existence*, p. 33.
[2] *Ibid.* p. 133.

His immanence He takes His share in the suffering; and God's share is, if I may use the phrase, the lion's share[1]." Again, one may observe that the sufferings of the world are not conceived of as, directly, God's own sufferings, but as sufferings with which He associates Himself by the fact of His immanence. So, later, Canon Streeter speaks of God as feeling the pain of others much more than we do, and as "bearing the suffering...in the right way[2]."

In the two most important contributions to the philosophy of religion and Christian theology which have been made by the Bishop of Manchester, *Mens Creatrix*[3] and *Christus Veritas*[4], the notion of suffering in God is accepted but it is presented as something which comes about in the course of the development of God's world-plan, and very definitely not as something which comes, as it were, upon God, and which God is compelled to endure. In *Mens Creatrix* Dr Temple describes all history as "the method of the Divine Love." He continues, "that love requires beings whom it may love, and requires their varying forms of evil for the perfecting of love. Inasmuch as it is love, it enters by sympathy into all pain and sorrow, and spends itself in the redemptive agony[5]." In *Christus Veritas* he points to the Agony and the Cross as showing "what selfishness in us means to God.... He displays his utter alienation from evil by showing us the pain that it inflicts on Him[6]." And in the chapter on "The Atonement" the

---

[1] *God and the Struggle for Existence*, p. 163.
[2] *Ibid.* pp. 177 f.   [3] 1917.   [4] 1924.
[5] *Mens Creatrix*, p. 290.   [6] *Christus Veritas*, p. 184.

same thought of the suffering caused to God by "the impact of sin[1]" recurs, while, beyond this, the Cross is viewed as "the unveiling of a mystery of the Divine Life itself—the revelation of the cost whereby God wins victory over the evil which He had permitted, and thereby makes more glorious than otherwise was possible the goodness which triumphs[2]." Towards the end of this chapter comes Dr Temple's fullest statement in connexion with the revelation of "new depths of the divine through the Atonement." "It was only in hesitating figures that men dared to conceive the suffering of God, until Christ died; and though the heart of man ached for the revelation of the Divine Passion, the philosophers would have none of it. Aristotle's 'apathetic God' was enthroned in men's minds, and no idol has been found so hard to destroy.... There is a highly technical sense in which God, as Christ revealed Him, is 'without passions'; for He is Creator and Supreme, and is never 'passive' in the sense of having things happen to Him except with His consent; also He is constant, and free from gusts of feeling carrying Him this way and that. His anger and His compassion are but the aspects of His holy love appropriate to varying circumstances. But the term really meant 'incapable of suffering,' and in this sense its predication of God is almost wholly false[3]." In a note Dr Temple explains his word "almost" by the fact that "it is truer to say that there is suffering in God than that God suffers." That there is suffering in God follows from the truth that God is revealed in Christ;

[1] *Christus Veritas*, p. 260. [2] *Ibid*. p. 262.
[3] *Ibid*. p. 269.

but the suffering "is always an element in the joy of the triumphant sacrifice."

Dr Temple puts the meaning of the element of suffering, particularly as manifested in Christ's passion and cross, very strongly: "no further entry of the Supreme God into the tangle and bewilderment of finitude can be conceived. All that we can suffer of physical or mental anguish is within the divine experience; He has known it all Himself. He does not leave this world to suffer while He remains at ease apart; all the suffering of the world is His[1]." But these words do not require, and pages in an earlier chapter "Eternity and History" forbid, us to suppose that Dr Temple's thought could find itself at home in Mr Rolt's delineation of God as "tied hand and foot in the midst of this evil world," owing to the nature of God's omnipotence. Nor is it easy to see how Mr Rolt could have accepted Dr Temple's account of the relation of God to the temporal world as most nearly paralleled in the work of the artist manipulating his material. Mr Rolt does indeed speak of God's eternal life of bliss in the mystery of the Holy Trinity, but of God's temporal relationship he could hardly have said with Dr Temple that God "remains outside the process, though it originates with Him and He guides it[2]."

The argument from God's love to God's suffering, with the revelation of God in Christ as the background and foundation, finds a place in two recent works that deal with Christology and soteriology. The first is *The*

[1] *Christus Veritas*, p. 270.
[2] *Ibid.* p. 188.

Incarnation of God[1] by the Rev. E. L. Strong, of the Oxford Mission to Calcutta. In it the author argues that but for the exaggerated doctrine of the transcendence of God, which passed into the Church from Judaism, it would long ago have been realized that the doctrine of the Incarnation involves the conviction that God "is one with us in all our experiences now, feels what we feel with us, and is always striving to get us to think and feel as He does. He lives man's life, that we may live His." It was not when He took man's nature that God was first moved by human sins and sorrows, but because God is love, and the nature of that love is manifested in Christ, we see that God's love is that of one "who perfectly enters into and sympathizes with all human life; one who is always affected by man's sins and sorrows." Christ's parables, in which He explains what the love of God is, "are pictures...of what God feels always—of what it is His eternal nature to feel[2]."

The second book alluded to above is by Dr Maldwyn Hughes, Principal of Wesley House, Cambridge, and bears the title *What is the Atonement? A Study in the Passion of God in Christ*[3]. One chapter is specially devoted to a discussion of suffering in God. It is partly an answer to a statement of the doctrine of impassibility by another Wesleyan theologian, Dr Marshall Randles, to which I shall shortly refer. Here it is Dr Hughes' own position which may be expounded. He insists that "we must choose whether or not we will accept the Christian revelation that 'God is love.' If we do, then we must

[1] Second edition, revised, 1920.
[2] *The Incarnation of God*, pp. 112 f.   [3] 1924.

accept the implications of the revelation....It is an entire misuse of words to call God our loving Father, if He is able to view the waywardness and rebellion of His children without being moved by grief and pity.... It is of the very nature of love to suffer when its object suffers loss, whether inflicted by itself or others. If the suffering of God be denied, then Christianity must discover a new terminology and must obliterate the statement 'God is love' from its Scriptures[1]." Dr Hughes goes on to argue that the idea of God as dynamic, not inactive, and the belief expressed by the word immanence, that "He enters into time and its experiences," point to the same conclusion: "the principle of suffering self-sacrifice is eternal in the Godhead[2]"; and, in time, God who is exalted above time "reacts to the experiences of the time-process[3]." So, in view of this truth, and of the truth that Christ was "a real incarnation of God," it is impossible to exclude the Deity in Christ from the sufferings which Christ endured: "our contention is not simply that Christ reveals a suffering God, but that the sufferings of Christ were the sufferings of God[4]." And as the Cross of Christ was not the beginning of the travail-sufferings of God, so, neither is it the end, but "by His Holy Spirit (which is the Spirit of Jesus) He is still travailing with men[5]."

[1] *What is the Atonement?* etc. pp. 92–4.
[2] *Ibid.* p. 95.   [3] *Ibid.* p. 98.
[4] *Ibid.* p. 102.   [5] *Ibid.* pp. 104 f.

CHAPTER III

Two Modern Criticisms of the Ascription of Passibility to God

W E have now observed in a number of modern writers a reaction against the doctrine of divine impassibility. That reaction has come from more than one quarter and has been marked by varying degrees of intensity. Contributions have been made from the side of philosophy as well as from that of distinctively Christian theology. Attention has been paid to the implications of the idea of creation as well as to the revelation of God's nature in the Person and sufferings of Christ. On the whole, the reaction has led to but little controversy. It has been commoner for the conception of passibility in God to be passed over in silence, or even excluded by inference, than to be directly assailed. In consequence, there is very little material on which to draw for the presentation in modern form of the ancient doctrine.

There is, however, one contribution to the subject in which that doctrine is defended at some length—Dr Marshall Randles' treatise entitled *The Blessed God. Impassibility*[1]. Dr Randles states the question in this form— whether the divine nature, *as such*, can be the subject of suffering. The view which he opposes seems to him to imply not only that "God undergoes painful passion," but also that "as He suffers in Himself all the depth and breadth of human pain, He is the greatest sufferer in existence." As against this "Our contention is that,

[1] 1900.

while abounding in mercy, as divine He is impassible[1]."
Stress is laid upon God's absolute perfection, and the
idea that inability to suffer involves God in limitation
is repudiated. If God suffered, His perfection would no
longer exist, since an element of evil would have a place
in His nature, for "whatever suffering may be in its
associations, uses or results, it is always *in se* an evil[2],"
and "no evil, not even non-moral, can be in Him who is
good in every conceivable respect and to whom no imperfection is possible[3]." Moreover, if there were suffering in God, He would not be, without reservation, the
blessed God; for the radical notion involved in speaking
of God as blessed is that of His happiness; and so "it
follows that lack of happiness is lack of blessedness, and
happiness mingled with unhappiness imperfect blessedness[4]": the Biblical doxologies are inconsistent with the
idea of a suffering God.

Dr Randles denies that the doctrine of impassibility
implies any lack of pity in God, or any aloofness. God,
the Blessed One, grapples closely with human misery,
"to counteract, reduce or annihilate it, without allowing
it to infect His nature or alloy His happiness[5]." We are
not compelled to associate suffering with God's pity and
sympathy in order to preserve their reality, nor is it true
that if the exalted Christ feels pain He is thereby brought
nearer to us; but "pity is a particular form of goodwill
or benevolence, and is not dependent for its existence on
the suffering of its subject[6]." Dr Randles holds together

---

[1] *The Blessed God. Impassibility*, p. 3.   [2] *Ibid.* p. 27.
[3] *Ibid.* p. 35.   [4] *Ibid.* p. 44.   [5] *Ibid.* p. 50.
[6] *Ibid.* p. 108.

belief in the richness of God's love and in the reality of the element of feeling in God, along with the refusal to admit that love and feeling involve passibility: "God," he writes, "is impassible, but not unfeeling; above all weakness and imperfection, but not icy intellect incapable of profound concern for the happiness of His creatures...If sympathy with the suffering means thought and benevolence concentrated upon him, the bending down of pity, intense concern to succour, sustain, relieve or deliver the child of adversity, compassion intent on doing all that is possible for the well-being of its needy object, the greatest of all sympathisers is the ever-blessed God." And such sympathy would not be worth more "by any admixture of pain[1]." And if the word "feeling" is used in the sense of "loving or not loving, approving or disapproving, delighting or not delighting in an object," then "God is a Being of pure and perfect feeling, out of which He cares for us as no other being can[2]." Such language as that of Isaiah lxiii, 9, in which God is spoken of as being afflicted, is "manifestly *poetic*." It teaches that God met the affliction of His people "as if it had acted through them against Himself, not that it impaired His infinite blessedness[3]." One more argument against the notion of passibility may be mentioned. Dr Randles believes that the prayers and worship of Christians cannot but be affected for the worse if this notion is entertained: "If His sympathetic pity for us involves His suffering on our account, our pity for Him as the greatest of all sufferers must involve

[1] *The Blessed God. Impassibility*, pp. 118 f.
[2] *Ibid.* p. 140.   [3] *Ibid.* p. 164.

our deep suffering on His account—a state of things which cannot but disturb and depress our feelings as we approach Him for worship and communion, and thus alloy what should be our purest bliss on earth or in heaven[1]."

That all suffering is *in se* evil, that the doctrine of divine passibility leads to the conclusion that God is the greatest of all sufferers and the object of man's pity, and that, therefore, the truth of God's blessedness is impaired, are all important elements in Dr Randles' argument. Dr Maldwyn Hughes challenges each of these positions. "It is very doubtful," he says, "whether every kind of suffering is to be described as 'evil.' Certainly that is not how we are wont to regard spontaneous and joyous self-sacrifice, or 'the passion for souls.'" Further, it is not necessary to conceive of God as "the most miserable object of our pity." For God is not helpless, a victim of circumstances, but "the Sovereign Lord who is on the throne." His suffering is the result of His voluntary self-limitation, and of His creation of beings who possess free-will. But He knows the end and has the joy of certainty as to the result of the travail of His soul. "He is not a finite God, who is struggling in the dark, and is uncertain as to the issue. Deeper than His suffering is His consciousness of the power of His will. This is the foundation of all blessedness, and this nothing can disturb[2]."

A criticism of the idea of passibility in God, much more recent than that of Dr Randles, but confined within

---

[1] *The Blessed God. Impassibility*, p. 176.
[2] *What is the Atonement?* pp. 91 f.

a few pages of one of the most interesting histories of the stages and developments in soteriological doctrine, appears in *Historic Theories of Atonement*[1] by Dr Robert Mackintosh. The criticism, as is the case with Dr Randles, is not directed against the belief that God can feel; on the contrary, as feeling exists in man, so there must be something analogous in God; "the noblest human feeling must point us to its source in God our Father, the God of love. A deity of stoical apathy is not the God whom Christ reveals." Where Dr Mackintosh differs sharply from Bushnell and later writers on the same side is when they come "to place suffering *qua* suffering in the psychosis of God Himself," and, in relation to atonement, conceive of God as suffering redemptively for sin long ages before His redeeming love was revealed on the plane of history in the Passion of Christ. Dr Mackintosh opposes to such views the assertion of God's happiness; "knowing the end from the beginning and seeing and feeling the whole as a whole—being in His inmost and deepest self the God of redemption—God possesses without effort or struggle the assurance that grace shall reign and that love must conquer. Therefore, in His calm vision of the unfolding ages, He must be happy indeed. An unhappy God would mean a bankrupt universe, a demonstrated pessimism, a doomed faith." It is to be noted that he is not content with the thought of God as possessing the assurance of final victory, and yet suffering in the course of the world-process for which the victory is not yet present. Any doctrine which imputes suffering to the divine nature

[1] 1920.

seems to him less than Christian. "We dare not," he writes, "impute suffering as suffering to the Most High. A God who fluctuates with changing circumstances, physical or human, is a Pagan god; and in the end that turns out to mean, No God at all." It was only in Christ that "Divine love now knew suffering as suffering," and there is no need to help out the Christian faith in the redemptive efficacy of Christ's sufferings by the thought of "age-long pain in heaven." On the contrary, to adopt such a belief is to drift into a Gnosticism in which the danger is of "losing a Christ who saves[1]."

[1] *Historic Theories of Atonement*, pp. 252–6.

CONCLUSION

I. MOTIVES PROMPTING THE ASSERTION OF DIVINE IMPASSIBILITY

THE historical evidence which has been brought together largely interprets itself. The ancient and medieval tradition of impassibility is bound up with three principal motives. There is, firstly, the motive which depends upon belief in the divine transcendence. Here, the dominant element in Hebrew thought as concerning God's relation to the world finds an ally in one powerful current of Greek thought, where the contrast between the One and the Many works itself out into a conception of God as aloof from the world, and possessing a life of His own which has no points of contact in respect either of purpose or of feeling with the life of the world. Then, secondly, there is the motive which arises out of the conviction that the life of God is a blessed life, and, as such, happy with the perfection of happiness. The idea that elements in the life of the world, in particular, the sufferings and the sins of men, could impair that blessedness of God, which seemed to arise out of the perfection of His own nature, would have been interpreted as allowing to the world a power to affect God's life, wholly incompatible with the belief in God's real independence of the world and in the bliss possessed by God in virtue of the eternal relationships of the divine Persons within the Godhead. And, thirdly, there is the motive which springs from the dread of anthropomorphism. The early Christian Fathers were no more backward than

Xenophanes had been in outspoken language concerning certain characteristics of Greek mythology. Those characteristics were part of that tradition whereby the Greek had assimilated the immortal gods to mortal men. This assimilation had taken full account of the element of feeling, and it was in the feelings which the poets had ascribed to the Olympians that these had shown themselves all too human. And even though not all Christian theologians might have followed Novatian and Arnobius in their view of the passions as corrupting the substance of him who gives way to them, they could not be easy with any interpretation of language concerning the emotional life of God which seemed to involve Him in the flow of changing and often irrational human passions.

Yet there were difficulties. The language of Scripture stood for, or symbolized, a real element in God's life. Love and wrath were in Him, whatever distinctions had to be made as safeguards against anthropomorphism. One could wish to know how far the method pursued by Augustine of making the feelings referred to in various parts of Scripture represent certain different characteristics of God's action was felt to be satisfactory. For behind and within any action of God there must be something which explains the action, and that "something" would seem necessarily to be connected with some kind of feeling-tone in God. Origen recognized this, as we saw, but without being able to work it into the texture of his theology. And then, there was the truth of the Incarnation and of the Cross. God was born, God suffered. As the forms of Christological thinking took more settled shape, it could be, and was said, "He suffered not as God, but as man; in the human nature, not in the divine." Yet, the sufferer was God; all the experiences, however endured, were experiences of the one Divine Person; and it was just because the Cross was not the Cross of a man, but of the Lord Jesus Christ, the Son of God made man, that the Cross saved. The Cross, at least, did not reveal an apathetic God, unconcerned for human woe. God, in Christ, had in some way descended from His blessedness. But beyond a certain point orthodox theology could not go. It could not make an adequate investigation of Patripassianism, or Monophysitism, to see whether any precious elements of truth might be involved in either heresy. That was not the method of those ages, and, indeed, in no age, while a struggle is actually taking place, is it easy to appreciate what may be the strong points in an opponent's position.

2. MOTIVES PROMPTING THE REACTION AGAINST THE DOCTRINE OF IMPASSIBILITY

The modern reaction against the doctrine of impassibility has not, in all its representatives, developed either from exactly the same presuppositions, or resulted in one closely-knit conception of the nature of God's relation to the world. Yet, here too, one may be confident of certain motives as at work. And, in the first place, the conclusions drawn from the Christian faith in God as Love must be emphasized. The thought that if God really loves, if His outgoing love is the expression of His innermost nature, then, confronted as He is with such a world as ours, He must suffer, is to be met with again and again among the opponents of the traditional doctrine. Their opposition amounted to a claim that the traditional doctrine had not been true to the one Christian standard, the revelation of God as Love, and that, therefore, the introduction of the notion of God's suffering was no adulteration of the true faith through the leaven of un-Christian thinking, but a loyal correspondence with the very core of true Christian thought about God.

Then, further, to not a few of those who agree in their dissent from the doctrine of impassibility, the character of the world, viewed as something which comes into being and develops its life through creative processes which reveal tension and costliness as present throughout the whole movement, suggests that the suffering of the world involves the suffering of God. The modern stress upon the doctrine of divine immanence has told in the same direction. The kind of conviction which has arisen at this point is that God could not be so closely associated with the world-process without sharing in those sufferings which are displayed at point after point in the history of the process, that a God who is really the ground of the world's being, the world being what it is, must be a suffering God.

And, thirdly, there are those to whom the Cross seemed to point backwards and inwards, back from the hill of Calvary into far-off aeons of the past, inwards, into the heart of God. What the Cross revealed in time —the Father giving the Son to redeem the world by suffering for it, that was eternally true of God's nature, and was always true in fact, ever since over against God, even though His work, a world existed. Thus, Calvary was the outward and visible sign, though far more than a sign, a true and efficacious sacrament, of a profound spiritual truth.

The modern reaction, then, starts from certain convictions as to God's nature and as to His relations with the world, just as the traditional view is unintelligible apart from another set of convictions directed towards the same fundamental realities. And because some, at least, of those different sets of convictions are, from the Christian standpoint, indubitably true, and would be affirmed on both sides of the argument as to impassibility, a constructive theology would need to aim at showing, if possible, how far a bridge could be built from the one side to the other, by the retention and use of all that was common to both sides.

3. SIX NECESSARY QUESTIONS

In order to make clearer what would be involved in an attempt to treat the notion of impassibility scientifically and to relate its truth, or the truth of the contrary notion, to a body of theological truth, the following six questions may be suggested, as necessary to discuss, and to answer with some degree of adequacy, before the problem of suffering in God can be at all satisfactorily dealt with.

The first question concerns the nature of God as the Absolute, as the ultimate reality, and, at the same time, as personal. It must make a difference to all that we go on to say in detail about God, whether we think of God as the Absolute, or as the supremest element within the Absolute. Is Professor Clement Webb right when he says, "the statement, in which recent philosophers of very various Schools in this country have concurred, that 'God is not the Absolute' must, I am sure, if seriously taken, make nonsense of Religion[1]"? If God and the Absolute are one, and religion and philosophy, though with different interests uppermost, are concerned with the same supreme reality, clearly we shall not be able to predicate finitude of God, with whatever consequences such finitude may naturally suggest, as something which appertains to Him in virtue of His being, not the Absolute, but within the Absolute. A God who is the Absolute will be a very different God from the one who has a home in Professor James' "Pluralistic Universe." And before we can make assertions of any value as to passibility or impassibility in God, we must be prepared to answer more fully the question: "What do you imply by the term 'God'?"

The second question follows close upon the first, and may be put in this way: "What is the true doctrine of God's relationship to the world, and, especially, with reference to creation?" Whatever exactly be involved in the idea of creation, the idea certainly includes the thought of God's priority to the world, as Cause to effect. If, then, God has brought the world into being, what does that mean for God? Is it true to say that He has limited Himself? If so, how far does such limitation extend? If God's relationship to creation as the continually sustaining power within creation is described as

---

[1] *God and Personality*, p. 153.

"immanence," how is that immanence, as truth, but
particular truth, to be understood in its bearing upon,
and in its dependence upon, the truth which stretches
beyond the idea of immanence? If we take the familiar
pair of notions—transcendence, immanence—as related
truths about the one God, what continuous meaning
does His transcendence have for His immanence, and
His immanence for His transcendence?

The third question follows out this question of God's
transcendent and immanent relationship to the world
into the conceivable consequences which it may have as
touching the contrast, yet not absolute separation, between eternity and time. So it may be asked "Can the
life of God be essentially blessed and happy, as being
that eternal life which cannot, as such, be in any way
affected by the time-series and its contents, and yet also
a life in which suffering finds a place, in so far as the life
of God enters into the time-series and works within it?"
Is the same sort of distinction legitimate, as between the
pure eternity of the divine life and the restrictions which
the time-series imposes upon that life, as the Bishop of
Manchester makes between the work of the Son of God
in the life recorded in the Gospels and the other work of
God, especially the work of providential care for the
world, which had been, and remained, His? Dr Temple
says, "the Incarnation is an episode in the Life or Being
of God the Son; but it is not a *mere* episode, it is a *revealing* episode[1]." Is the whole of God's work, when
that work has to be thought of in terms of time, an
episode, and yet a revealing episode? The question con-

[1] *Christus Veritas*, p. 144.

cerns the reasonableness of believing that passibility is not an intrinsic truth of the divine nature, but a truth which comes into being through, and expresses a certain aspect of, the condescension of the Absolute to the contingent, of the Eternal to the things of time.

The fourth question is directed to the meaning to be attached to feeling, and to suffering as a species of feeling within God. "How," one may ask, "is feeling in God related to feeling in men? And is there a particular kind of feeling properly describable as suffering, and experienced as suffering by God?" The evidence to which attention has been directed in historical study does little to throw light upon this most important question. It is much easier to form a picture of what thinking and willing mean, when ascribed to God, than of what feeling means. Thought and will seem to have a meaning when used in connexion with God who is Spirit which cannot be equally truly said of feeling. This general difficulty about feeling becomes particular in reference to suffering. Have we any means of representing to ourselves the character of the experience by God of continuous and acute suffering in time? Our difficulty at this point does not carry with it the conclusion that the whole conception of a suffering God, or of suffering in God, is essentially absurd. If man is made in the image of God, and it is through what we know of human personality that we find the best way of conceiving of the life and nature of God, then something which is linked up so closely with the whole of human life as is the element of feeling has, presumably, some archetypal perfection of itself existing in God.

Even if "feeling," owing to its associations, is an unfortunate word, it still may be much truer to say that God feels than that He does not. Whether those feelings can ever be described as sufferings is a question not simply as to the credibility of unpleasantly-toned emotion being experienced by God, but also as to the moral associations connected with the idea of suffering.

So we move on to the fifth question: "Is a real religious value secured in the thought of the possibility of God?" It makes much difference whether, given the notion of a suffering God, God is thought of as suffering because the world leaves Him no option, in which case God's nature must be regarded as rendered passible by the constraint exercised upon it by the world, or whether God is said to suffer because in His love He freely associates Himself with the world's suffering by means of a true compassion. So one might bring in another of theology's relatively valuable distinctions, and ask whether God suffers because of His nature, or because of His grace. There is, indeed, no truth concerning God's nature which lacks religious value. The metaphysical attributes, so uncongenial to William James, have, I think, far more religious and devotional worth than he recognized. Nevertheless, when we think of God's grace, we think especially of what God does for the world and man, which, being apprehended by man, becomes the rich material out of which the religious life of thankfulness, response and effort is built up. If God suffers, is that part of His graciousness, for which our thanks are due to Him? And if it is part of His graciousness, what exactly is secured by it? Is it the knowledge that God is with us in all the toils and endurances of life, in its difficulties and sorrows and losses? Is the alternative to a suffering God an unsympathetic God? Or can man be sure that God gives him richly all that he needs, that God never passes by on the other side like the priest in the parable, nor simply comes and looks, like the Levite, but is ready, with everything that the oil and wine symbolize, to raise man from his evil plight; —and yet believe that "suffering" is the wrong word to use about God, and that if God suffered, man would be none the better for it? It is a matter for fuller examination than has been given it, whether, from the human point of view, the fact of God's happiness or the fact of God's suffering would better secure the highest values which man desires to find present in the Universe and determinative of its character.

And then, as to the sixth and final question. We may put it in some such way as this: "What is the relationship of the Cross as the historic means of God's redemption of the world to that eternal background of God's love out of which the Cross is given?" That the Cross reveals in a supreme way the love of God and His redemptive will is a belief common to Christians who in many ways would differ widely from one another. But it is another matter when the Cross is regarded as the projection on to the plane of history of something, namely redemptive suffering, which is eternal truth about God's nature. Questions as to the connexion between eternity and time, and as to the specific quality of redemption, in Christian thought, as involving atonement, must be faced before the Passion of the Cross can be interpreted as the historic counterpart of a Passion ever living in the heart of God. The significance of the Cross cannot be confined within the limits of time, but it does not follow that the actual pain of the Cross can be transferred backwards into the life of God and viewed as always associated with His love. There arises a theological issue as to the nature of the Christian Gospel, which needs to be treated with much care.

When, into the assertion or rejection of any doctrine, there enters a fervour of feeling, and the conviction that the debate and strife range round no mere *theologoumenon*, but round a faith which creates and sustains spiritual life and hope, it is at least probable that something which really makes a difference to man's conception of the nature and character of God is at stake. But when this is so, it is not the less necessary that the subject under dispute should be viewed in its context of history, philosophy, and theology, that, when decisions are made, this should be after a survey of the whole field, and not through preoccupation with one corner of it. A survey so comprehensive is not made in this present study; it may, perhaps, be of use as an indication of the need, and as a stimulus to its satisfaction.

INDEX

For EU product safety concerns, contact us at Calle de José Abascal, 56–1°,
28003 Madrid, Spain or eugpsr@cambridge.org.

www.ingramcontent.com/pod-product-compliance
Ingram Content Group UK Ltd.
Pitfield, Milton Keynes, MK11 3LW, UK
UKHW020316140625
459647UK00018B/1900